Maxyne G.

BA, RPR, CRR, CCR

WAY OFF THE RECORD

A collection of experiences of some of the nation's most well-respected court reporters, ranging from the hilarious to the horrific, and everything in between!

WAY OFF THE RECORD

By Maxyne G. Bursky

Copyright © 2011 by Maxyne G. Bursky

Cover photograph by Jena Golden Photography

Cover design by Kip Williams, Print-Ink Press

Have a story of your own that you would like to see in the next edition of **Way Off The Record**? Contact Maxyne at Maxyne@MaxyneBursky.com or call 770.320.7780

Other books by Maxyne G. Bursky:

Talk to the Hands!

The *Term*-inator

Good Dogs with Bad Names

ISBN: 978-0-9821555-2-3

0-9821555-2-2

Dedicated to my dear brother

HAL BRIEN SPERGEL

whose love, wit, courage, and talent have
inspired me my entire life

Author Acknowledgement

The following court reporting professionals have graciously contributed their time, their experience, and their talent to make this book a reality, for which I am forever grateful:

Deanna P. Baker

Lisa Barrett

Regina Berenato-Tell

Jack Boenau

Doreen C. Borgmann

Richard Bursky

Karen Carney-Giles

William Cohen

Marlene "Hedy" Coleman

Dianne Coughlin

Theresa Marie Crowder

Beulah Dalrymple

Daniel Feldhaus

Vicki LW Hartmetz

Patty Lee Hubble

Joseph Inquagiato

Roy Isbell

Thomas J. Kresse

Carmelita Lee

Gene Lee

Rick Levy

Kenneth McClure

Kelly McKee

Barbara J. Memory

Thomas W. Murray

Tori Pittman

Charlotte C. Roche

Merilyn Sanchez

Sheri Smargon

Susie Salenger Smith

Jacqueline M. Timmons

Michelle Vitrano

Donald J. White

Table of Contents I

Table of Contents II

Table of Contents III

The reader should note that all names in the stories that follow have been changed to protect the individuals' privacy, with the exception of participants in cases and courts that are already in the public domain.

Angels Among Us?

By Maxyne G. Bursky, BA, RPR, CRR, CCR

The deponent was a middle-aged woman with short, tousled, salt-and-pepper hair. I was already dreading the assignment, as the witness' replies to her attorney in the reception area of the law firm were being delivered quickly, in staccato-like fashion, consistently overtalking him.

Once we were all ushered into the conference room, I quickly set up, and we began. I was pleasantly surprised by the change in the deponent's demeanor. The preliminary questions and answers moved smoothly, orderly, almost classically – until the questioner, Mr. Jones, began to delve more substantially into the circumstances of the case.

This was a medical malpractice suit, with Ms. Smith, the witness, suing on behalf of her minor son, a teenager, who had suffered brain damage during the course of what was characterized as a routine appendectomy. The allegation was that during the course of the operation, the anesthesiologist had not properly monitored the administration of the anesthetic gases.

As counsel began to inquire about the boy's condition preoperatively, Ms. Smith fell silent, eyes closed, right hand slowly rising until fully extended toward the ceiling. I recall thinking to myself, a line from an old Bette Davis movie: "Fasten your seatbelts, it's going to be a bumpy night."

After a pause of literally three minutes, with Ms. Smith frozen in this position, Mr. Jones asked, "Ma'am, are you all right? If you're feeling ill, we can take a break."

Her eyes shot open, fixed on her interrogator, hand still in the air: "Hush! The angels are speaking! You'll get your answer as soon as they get done." Eyes shut again. More silence.

Mr. Miller, the witness' attorney, merely shrugged his shoulders and sat mute – but seemingly not dumbfounded, as Jones and I were. Apparently this was not Miller's first rodeo with this client. But Jones, unprepared for such depo-drama, insisted we recess so that her attorney could confer with her – and possibly her angels – regarding the developing bizarre character of the testimony.

During the break, I took the opportunity to edit what little data I had on my computer screen, and add the cover and appearance pages to the file, as was my habit during breaks in testimony. A good half hour had passed and we had still not reconvened. Mr. Jones poked his head in to see whether the deponent and her lawyer had returned, but they had not yet materialized.

At that point, I figured I'd just pop into the restroom and then return to the conference table. Murphy's Law as it relates to court reporters dictates that as soon as the reporter leaves the deposition room, that's when all the parties show up, ready to go.

As I pushed open the door of the ladies' lounge, my heart sank. There was Ms. Smith, standing by the sinks, right arm pointing skyward, eyes crammed shut. She was arguing rapid-fire with – the angels? There was nobody else in there but us chickens.

Just as I was gently retreating to the door to make my silent escape, her eyes flashed open, and stamping her foot, she exclaimed, "What should I do? The angels are telling me one thing and he" – *her attorney?* – "is telling me something else!"

I was frozen. She launched into an expletive-laced critique of her heavenly advisors as well as her legal ones that was both frightening and sad. As she paused to take a breath, I quickly mumbled something incomprehensible and headed out of the ladies' room and straight to reception. Smith's tirade was clearly audible, even though I stood 25 feet from the closed restroom door.

Long story a bit shorter, security and, soon thereafter, paramedics were summoned, and Ms. Smith was removed. I learned later from Mr. Jones that adjustments were made to the suit, and another plaintiff representative was chosen.

Reporting in the Far East

By Lisa Barrett, RPR, CRR, CSR

After 29 years of reporting in every venue imaginable, it was time to make a change. I had spent the past few years in pharmaceutical patent litigation. Some of the bioorganic chemical names do not even fit on one line of transcript. There are plenty of pharmaceutical patent lawyers in Canada who have multiple degrees in chemistry, chemical engineering, as well as law. They are totally unaware that there is a record being made. Their speeds are crazy, the chemical names are crazy. I thought, if I can do this and be nailing it — it's time for a new challenge. Hence came the idea into my head: Let's see how far in the world this job can take me.

Next step, I checked out Asia. Although Toronto is more cultured than most cities: three Chinatowns, Greek

Town, Little Italy, Little Portugal, India Village, I felt it was time in my career to embrace another culture, in a deep and meaningful way.

I was offered work in Singapore in 2008, while on an assignment that took me there as well as to Hong Kong. My husband and I decided this would be the adventure of a lifetime, and we sold our house. We left for Singapore on August 21, 2009. It was just the two of us – we left our 20- and 23-year-old kids safely nestled in Ontario.

The learning curve in court reporting in Singapore was huge. The demographic is about 50 percent Chinese, 30 percent Malay, and 20 percent Indian. Although English is the first language in Singapore, they speak "Singlish." This is a combination of Chinese and English which is really difficult to understand. Singaporeans use a lot of slang as well. For example, the word *"ex"* means "expensive." They say *"lah"* a few times during every sentence.

Then there are all the British spellings and punctuation one needs to pick up – quickly. All the formatting was British as well, so no periods after Mr. or Mrs.; no Z's in any words ("analyse"); and the questions and judge's speech were "cleaned up," as you write, a concept I was unfamiliar with, since I had always been a literal verbatim reporter.

I worked with an editor, who sat in the courtroom with me and edited from my screen. I used LiveNote software in order to watch my own writing on my computer monitor. Oftentimes we would share-write, and split the takes up with another reporter all day, like runners in a relay race, passing the baton back and forth.

The company I worked for expected complete perfection within the first week of my arrival. Hah! I was a 29-year veteran of verbatim reporting and, now, I had to edit on the fly and remove all the extraneous words said by counsel and the judge. Instead of, "I got off the bus," I would learn to write, "I alighted the bus."

The transcripts had to be churned out to perfection within three hours of completion of court proceedings. There were production people at the office waiting for them. This was how I worked every day. We had editors who worked with us in the courtroom. Some of the editors called themselves reporters as well. We were called input reporters and the editors were called output reporters.

I worked five days a week, and usually did not arrive home until 7:30 – 9:00 each night. It was pretty grueling, but in hindsight, that routine has made my writing so much better. I feel that I can now take on any assignment with complete confidence.

The Supreme Court in Singapore is a $600 million building that entirely covers a large city block. There are approximately 16 courtrooms in this building.

Courts do not proliferate here; Singapore is almost crime-free. A fellow reporter put her cigarette butt in a hedge one day and a man followed her to the courtroom, got her name and employment and went and reported her to the police. As a result, she was fined $300!

People are still caned in Singapore. A whipping mechanism with hooks on it literally tears the skin wide open. You are promptly driven to the hospital to get stitched up, and returned to the jail. If you receive a sentence of four canings, you have your choice of whether to get them all at once, or one per month. The caning is on your buttocks. If you appeal your sentence in Singapore and you lose (which is extremely likely to occur), you will get double your original sentence.

People are still hanged in Singapore. This can occur for literally any amount of illicit drugs the accused happened to be peddling. Hanging also occurs for murder or illegal possession of firearms.

Justice is swift. I heard about people being charged and hanged within a month. The hangings occur on Friday and have been done by the same Indian man, Darshan Singh, since 1959, who declares to the convicted, "I am going to send you to a better place than this. God bless you."

While I lived in Singapore, we had a two-bedroom flat on the main floor in a big complex on East Coast, about 15 minutes outside of the city, very close to the waterfront on the South China Sea. Singapore is the biggest shipping port in Asia, so with the steady stream of ships, the water is polluted and you aren't able to swim. We ate dinner daily at the "hawker stalls," usually soups or chicken and rice.

We tried to cook, but because one portion of our condo was completely exposed to the outside, with no glass, we didn't bother turning on the air conditioner, and with 90-degree F temperatures, we weren't about to start heating up the place more. We didn't drive for 13 months either. We used bicycles.

Public transportation was far more harrowing than in Toronto! In one instance, my ride was almost turbulent. The driver desperately clung to the wheel as the bus rounded the sharp Singapore highway curve with a blown-out tire. I was sitting in the front of the bus, and I could see in the side mirror that the tire was completely on fire. My first thought was: "I'll be trapped on this bus and it will explode." It didn't help that I am terrified of fire.

As the bus screeched to a stop, a fellow passenger demanded to be let off. The driver opened the door for him, and I quickly followed. There were only about six of us who left the crowded bus. As I walked beside the speeding cars on the narrow strip of a shoulder, I visualized next all those drivers, talking away on their cell phones, repeatedly, and unknowingly, running me over.

At one point, in order to reach the grassy area bordering the highway, I had to dart across two lanes of oncoming cars. On a regular morning in Singapore, the temperature is around 90 degrees F. After dashing across the highway, my entire blouse was drenched in sweat. Good thing I had left my writer in the courtroom, and was only carrying my laptop. Fortunately, I was able to grab another bus and arrived at the Supreme Court of Singapore unscathed.

I got to travel to Bangkok twice to do US depos. It was amazing. My husband went elephant riding; I worked. The attorneys were super-nice, and we were served smoothies in champagne glasses in the morning in the depo room. Pure luxury. The hotel was opulent and even had real orchids on the elevators.

I was also able to go to Phuket, Thailand twice on vacation. I have worked in Hong Kong several times as well. Hong Kong is simply an amazing place. I could easily write another story just on Hong Kong and my amazing experiences there. I also spent two days in Taiwan, where I was completely surprised to find so North American: cars are on the right side of the road, and the electricity voltage is the same.

The best part of working in Singapore was meeting the most amazing court reporters I have ever had the honor to work with. One particular reporter, Helen Case, started reporting in Australia at age 16. She owned her first house at age 18. She has worked everywhere in the world, even Rwanda. She's a bit of an adrenaline junkie, like me.

I have so many dear friends as a result of my global adventures. It's different when you're all working in a foreign country like that; friendships are made quickly and they're invaluable. I am still in touch almost weekly with my kindred-spirited international court reporter buddies.

I am very lucky to have chosen this career and I am so grateful for all the places that court reporting has been able to take me in my lifetime and the wonderful experiences I have had and the amazing people I have met along the way.

Lisa Barrett, RPR, CRR, CSR, started reporting in 1979 at County Court in Toronto, Ontario, Canada and spent 11 years there, doing mostly criminal trials, about 60 percent jury. She left Toronto in 1990 and moved to a small rural town in Ontario, Canada, working in a one-room courthouse for two years and then back in court in two different towns.

In 1995 she opened a reporting firm with a partner, owning that business for 12 years. Two years later, Lisa accepted a reporting contract in Singapore, which lasted 13 months.

Returning home in September of 2010, she now works for Neeson & Associates in Toronto, providing CART, captioning, and reporting of all types.

Vignette 1: A Moving Experience

By Jack Boenau, RPR, CRR, CBC, CCP, RDR, FAPR

Another court reporter that I had worked with, Joe, had a moving experience in court... literally. A judge, who didn't like to be on record for certain comments that he would make, instructed the court reporter to stop writing at that point in the proceedings.

Previously, the attorneys had all agreed that *everything* must be on the record, and the reporter was not to stop typing no matter what. Startled to see Joe still pounding the keys, the judge repeated his demand. Nevertheless, Joe kept doing what he was there to do.

Finally, the frustrated judge ordered two bailiffs to carry him out of the room. Undaunted, the reporter lifted his knees, keeping the steno machine firmly in place, and he continued writing until he was physically deposited out of hearing range.

Jack Boenau, RPR, CRR, CBC, CCP, RDR, FAPR, trained under Thyra D. Ellis, a convention reporter in Jacksonville, Florida, and started traveling the country reporting for her before he was old enough to rent a car. He then worked with Frank Sarli in Orlando as a

freelancer/deputy official, then took a traveling officialship in Iowa, eventually moving back home to Sarasota, Florida, as a freelance owner where he got back into convention reporting, CART and captioning in the late 80s.

Jack was the first person to caption at the National Court Reporters Association (then National Shorthand Reporters Association) convention in 1989, and provided realtime translation to the World Wide Web for Vice-President Al Gore's speech on "The Information Superhighway."

Jack started AmeriCaption and is working seven days a week (because that's all there are) after more than 40 years on the keyboard.

What's in a Name?

By Karen Carney-Giles, RPR, CMRS, CSR

Since my journey as a court reporter began on my home turf, New York City...the Big Apple...that is the setting for my story. New York City is a melting pot of people and personalities, and I've worked with the good, the bad, and "the uglies."

To set the stage: I was on a realtime job with a colleague of mine, Mary, whom I enjoy partnering with because of her unique combination of camaraderie and professionalism. We work well together, share the same work ethic, and sense of humor. We also each possess very sharp tongues...a result of our territory.

It was a Monday morning and the beginning day of discovery in what would turn out to be protracted litigation. The attorneys required multiple hookups and final copy at the end of the day. There was a room full of attorneys, with paralegals in tow.

At the time of this deposition, computer-aided transcription software was not as sophisticated as it is today. You couldn't edit on the fly, a practice which now makes for a more accurate appearance on the lawyer's monitor. Hence, it was beneficial to take a team approach. I was doing the realtime reporting, with my colleague editing.

After gathering the appearance information, defining speakers, hooking up the attorneys' computers, the proceedings commenced. For the first half hour during the preliminary questioning, everything was going smoothly.

Suddenly, the atmosphere began to radically change. As the questioning became more involved, one defense counsel, Mr. Smith, started objecting to almost every question. Things started getting very heated. The questioning counsel, Mr. Jones, requested that Mr. Smith stop making speeches; to just say "objection."

Prolonged colloquy ensued. At last, the combative attorneys came up for air. There was a brief silence while all counsel appeared to regroup. During the pause, Mr. Smith glanced at his computer screen and became red-faced. He then stated for the record that the reporter made an error; that his name is Mr. Smith, not Mr. Van Dyke.

My reporting partner piped up with a request to go off the record. She explained that we were aware of the problem and that the mistranslate was coming from a designation of counsel from a previous case that had gotten into my master dictionary. Mary assured him that the correction would be made during a break. Mr. Smith was satisfied with the explanation – or so it seemed.

We went back on the record. Mr. Smith continued in an obstreperous fashion with incredibly verbose objections. Suddenly, he was gesturing via some esoteric sign language, wildly pointing at his computer screen. "Mr. Van Dyke" was in the realtime transcript again!

I've got to tell you that my colleague is a gem. Interpreting his message correctly, she replied in similar sign language that we had a handle on the problem.

Again, her response seemed to fall "on deaf hands."

Mr. Smith again made a statement on the record about his true identity. Other counsel exchanged exasperated looks and began rolling their eyes.

Finally, a recess was taken. Before anyone had the opportunity to get up, Mr. Smith made his way around the conference table to our side and doggedly pointed out the well-known fact that his name is not Mr. Van Dyke.

Everyone has their limits – even court reporters. I smiled from ear to ear and replied, "Mr. Smith, at this point you're lucky that's all we're calling you."

The heretofore-somber deposition participants erupted in laughter, and Mr. Smith finally seemed to get the message. As he left the room to take a break, Mary and I grinned at each other, knowing justice was served this day.

Karen Carney-Giles, CSR, RPR, CMRS, is a partner in Fink & Carney Reporting and Video Services. She began her freelance court reporting career in 1971. Karen has lectured on both a local and national level on court reporting, legal support services, and the

importance of court reporters maintaining impartiality.

She has served as a board member, chair and president of the New York State Court Reporters Association, and has worked on NCRA's CMRS Committee and the Citizens for Impartial Justice Board.

She is married to Colin Giles and lives in New York City, where both maintain an active lifestyle. Karen has completed five marathons and competes on a regular basis in races sponsored by the New York Road Runners Club.

The Slip and Fall Expert

By Thomas W. Murray, RPR

It was realtime to the judge, and my turn to relieve the acting reporter. My writer was hooked up to the computer by an extra-long wire so I could move around the courtroom with the machine during jury selection, and cover the sidebar without unplugging. This, of course, was before remote connections had been perfected. The judge's computer was connected with a rather short wire, but it was sufficient. I was prepared for everything and anything the trial could throw at me — or so I thought.

Blank stares of judge and jury at one point during the proceedings told me that the assemblage was hearing the testimony but not listening. My partner John stopped his translation as I approached and collegially started mine. Satisfied that things were in order, he picked up his writer and began to leave for the transcription room.

I laughed to myself as John's substantial silhouette blocked my view of the document projected on the screen. I stopped laughing when I saw my connecting wire wrapped around his ankle.

In a flash, a reporter's nightmare assaulted my brain: with all eyes now on John's backside, brightly illuminated by the beam of the document projector, the wire would quickly tighten around his ankle; I would valiantly dive to catch my writer before it, too, toppled; I would fail at same; and poor John would trip, landing head first against counsel table!

I had to act quickly. I was desperate. A thought balloon popped into my imagination, but alas, it was empty of text. As all hope for a graceful way out began to quickly vanish, I decided to act now and think later. In the middle of the droning testimony, I yelled out, "JOHN!!"

The eyes of the startled judge, jury, and attorneys were all on me. "THE WIRE!!" I bellowed. I had to finish what I had started. I wildly pointed to the potentially offending apparatus.

Startled as well, John looked down, muttered a dull, "Oh," freed his ankle from the wire, and continued out of the courtroom. With a sheepish grin, I said, "Sorry," to no one in particular. There was an awkward silence as court personnel and lay participants looked at each other.

After what I perceived to be an eternity, and without comment on the incident, the judge said sardonically, "Continue, counsel," and the examination resumed. Needless to say, however, I was forced to endure some amount of ribbing from my fellow reporters ranging from sage advice on the proper handling of wires in the courtroom, to tongue-in-cheek inquiries regarding my desire to use whatever means necessary to keep my colleague in the proceedings longer than he wanted or needed to be there!

Thomas W. Murray, BS, RPR, began as a freelance court reporter in New York City in 1974, armed with a bachelor of science in economics from New York University.

Tom became an official in the United States District Court for the Southern District of New York in 1988, and intends to continue there until retirement. Thus far, he declares the Martha Stewart trial as the best assignment ever.

Tom enjoys living in the Chinatown section of Manhattan. His current hobbies are tap and ballroom dancing, sailing, and bowling (yes, really).

Fun and Games with Nepotism

By Maxyne G. Bursky, BA, RPR, CRR, CCR

This story, although authored by me, comes from a reporter who wishes to be anonymous. Now retired, he was a freelancer in an area of the country where official reporters, due to varying circumstances, were not bound to make a record of every trial in their court. As a result, attorneys could bring someone in from an outside agency to take down proceedings and produce transcript.

Jerry Schwartz (not his real name, of course) was assigned to report a trial in which one of his clients, a rather large law firm with several named partners, was representing the defendants. Jerry saw several associates on the signature page of the notice of trial, and was amused when the lead attorney was a Michael

Schwartz (not his real name, of course, but the namesake *was* real).

Ordinarily, this coincidence would have created a 30-second banter between counsel and reporter, but this proceeding was destined for a lot more hilarity than that.

The judge presiding over the case happened to be the Honorable Stephen Schwarz (pronounced the same as the names of the other two court officers previously mentioned, albeit spelled without the T). Even so, perhaps a minute could be allotted to this amusing scenario, but for the fact that Jerry, Michael and Stephen shared the same rapier-sharp wit.

Attorney Daniel Jones, representing the plaintiff, entered the courtroom a few minutes after the first three had wrung what Jerry thought was the last drop of amusement out of this name game. But he hadn't reckoned on what was to happen next.

As Mr. Jones was organizing his papers at counsel table, Michael walked up to him and politely introduced himself. Jerry distributed his business cards to all counsel and the clerk, as was his custom.

Mr. Jones suddenly stopped what he was doing and said with a smile, "Hey, how about that. Everybody is named Schwartz except for myself – and the parties!"

With all the deadpan he could muster, Judge Schwarz looked at Jerry and said, "So how's Mom? Everybody okay at home?"

Not missing a beat, Michael chimed in, "Jerry's daughter Robin was in from college, so we had a barbecue. She said to say 'Hi, Uncle Steve.'"

"That's right, I forgot," continued the jurist, completely deadpan. "Sorry I missed it. I was out of town this weekend. Poker night still on for Friday?"

"Of course," responded Jerry. "Only Mike brings the cigars this time." Michael chuckled and nodded.

Plaintiff's counsel, while striving to maintain his composure, seemed to be struggling. The blood seemed to be draining from Daniel Jones' face.

After a momentary silence, all three Schwartz "relatives" burst out laughing, unable to restrain themselves. Judge Schwarz took pity on Jones and, as self-appointed commander of the obvious, patiently explained that the name coincidence was too great a vehicle to pass up for a mild practical joke. It was a great way to start the week (at least according to Stephen, Michael and Jerry)!

The Towering QwestFerno

By Vicki LW Hartmetz, RPR, CMRS, CLVS, CRI, CPE, CSR, FAPR

Periodically during my 36-year career, I have joined the ranks of the freelance world. While reporting in court has been my mainstay, I have dabbled in the nooks and crannies of our profession and always enjoyed all facets of my experience.

During one of my freelance stints, I worked for a firm in Colorado. Our family had recently moved to the Denver area and our children were young then, so freelancing seemed to fit our schedules easily. I had just invested in my first PC-based CAT system and was quickly building my dictionary and relearning the ropes of transcription. I reported all over the metro area, learning the lay of the land. I was having fun, and it was a great time in my career.

One of my most memorable depositions was set for two days, to be taken in the USWest building downtown. Of course, USWest was once Mountain Bell and was then Qwest, if you're keeping track, as telecommunications companies come and go down the line.

The building was 48 stories tall and quite a prominent part of the skyline. At that time, I didn't realize that many skyscrapers are built with some "give" so that when the wind blows, they sway to a small extent. I soon found that the USWest building was one of those architectural wonders.

When I arrived for the first day of the job in an employer/employee dispute, the weather was blustery to the point that dust was clearly visible up on the 46th floor in the USWest general offices. I stood looking out the window in the glass tower. I may have had an apprehensive look on my face, because one of the administrators assured me that, yes, the building was teetering slightly in the wind, but not to worry; it was intended that way.

The deposition was taken in an inside conference room, so we spent the day without the benefit of windows while we listened to the wind whistling and the building groaning as it swayed. The time went by quickly, thankfully, and the attorneys decided to call it a day a little after 5:30 in the evening. The weather hadn't improved — at least from the sounds the building was making and the howling of the wind.

I began to pack up my equipment, and when I was ready to head to the elevator, I decided to take a minute to call my agency and check in. While talking to the office manager, the lights suddenly went out. You know, it's amazing how dark an inside conference room can be without electricity.

I searched in the dark for my purse and machine case. *Great,* I thought, my first purchase will be one of those little key ring flashlights so I'm prepared next time (I did buy it, but never used it)! Just about the time I found my way through the maze of chairs to my belongings, the fire alarm began to sound. *Great,* I thought, here I was in a building that I had never been in before 8:00 that morning in the dark, and now we were having a fire drill.

I made my way to the door. You'd think the entire world simply disappeared at 5:00. There was absolutely no one to be seen in the hallways. The emergency lights were coming on, but not the building's power. I cautioned myself to stay calm; it was probably just a false alarm. Finally, a man came around the corner and said I should leave the building; that he didn't know what was going on, but he couldn't be sure that there wasn't a fire somewhere. Then he was gone.

Well, I'll have you know that I had seen *The Towering Inferno* the previous weekend on the Classic Weekend Movie and wasn't about to let my little boys be orphans. I took a deep breath, picked up my machine case, and headed for the stairway – high heels and all!

Maybe I didn't think things through as calmly as I should, but there was no one around, and I thought that 92 flights of stairs (two per floor) would be a good alternative to sitting in the dark or succumbing to smoke inhalation. The phones were no longer working (typical for a telecommunications office) and setting off seemed like the most logical step to take.

This was pre-9/11, and little did I know that once I started down the stairs, I couldn't get onto other floors without a pass card or code to open doors. *Great security,* I thought. Around the 35th floor, another human being actually got on the staircase with me. He was moving as fast as he could. He said the rumor was there was a fire on the 33rd floor and it was a good idea to keep going. I picked up my pace as I went past the door on the 33rd floor. I didn't see any smoke, much less smell any, but there was a haze of some sort in the stairwell.

As I continued down into the 20s, an entire group of people passed me. They were in too much of a hurry to stop and chat. Then there was the sound of a loud speaker instructing everyone to stay calm; that investigators were on the 25th floor searching for the source of the alarm. *Great,* I thought, as I looked at the locked door with the number 25 written on it. I kept trudging down the stairs.

By this time, I was losing my enthusiasm for the whole project. My machine case was heavy, but I was too protective of my new SmartWriter to simply leave it on the stairs, and yet, I was determined to make it out of that building, no matter what. I tightened my grip on the handle of the case and the strap of my purse (which was no small bag during those years) and plodded on.

When I reached the 10th floor, something was being said over the building speakers again, but I couldn't make out what it was. I could be heading into the inner sanctum of the fire and I'd never know it. The time had come, though, when I was promising God that if I lived through this ordeal, I'd get in shape so that I could do 92 flights of stairs without breaking a sweat.

Lo and behold, the last flight was before me. I had seen no one since the 18th floor and the emergency lights still glowed. I threw the door open and found myself on the far side of the lobby. Fire trucks were pulling away from the front doors and some firemen were still on scene. I heard as I passed them that there had not been a real fire, but smoke in an electrical box. As for the power, that had been a result of the constant wind that day, and the juice would soon return.

Great, I thought, I'll still have to come back tomorrow. Oh, well, at least I was safe, even if my legs felt like lead. I did return the next day and we finished the deposition by noon. Of course, the pain in my legs was intense, especially the day after my experience.

I did take solace in the fact that, had I been a minute earlier, I would have ridden down in the elevator. The parties, attorneys, and deponent were all in the same elevator car when the power went out. It was over two hours before they reached the first floor. *Great,* I smiled to myself. I'm glad I missed that joyride!

Vicki LW Hartmetz, RPR, CSR-KS, CMRS, CLVS, CRI, CPE, FAPR, has been a court reporter since 1975. Most of her career has been spent in court as an official, 31 years, although she has experience in most every aspect of judicial and freelance reporting. She is currently an official in Centennial, Colorado.

An established author, Vicki has been a contributing editor to the NCRA's Journal of Court Reporting for many years and has published dozens of articles. She has completed two books in her own right: **Court Tales,** *a collection of sometimes amusing experiences from court work, and* **Red Letter Days,** *the inspiring story of quadriplegic Kevin Wolitzsky. Vicki's younger son served two tours of duty in Iraq, which prompted the current family project, a book which they have named* **In the Silence that Follows,** *which explores the malady of post-traumatic stress disorder and not only what happens to the soldier, but to the family left behind.*

A Day in Haiti

By Rick Levy, BBA, RPR, FPR

I do not remember the year, but it was in either 2001 or 2002. The office got a call for an assignment in Port-au-Prince, Haiti. It was called in as a short, three-hour deposition, which meant we would leave Florida in the morning and arrive back home that same day.

There were actually two depos of a couple of family members of a Haitian national who had been working in Miami and had had a fatal accident. The attorneys needed to depose them about the type of financial assistance that the deceased had been sending back home over the years.

The two attorneys, the Creole interpreter, and I boarded the plane at Miami Airport that morning. The plan was to arrive at noon, drive an hour, take the two depos and return on a scheduled 5:00 p.m. flight.

When we landed in Haiti, we caught a cab, with the tremendous help of our Creole interpreter. We drove through Port-au-Prince and witnessed the reality of a Third World country, with houses half built, school buses with kids hanging off the sides, and people carrying fruits and vegetables on their shoulders and heads.

The examinations took place at a hotel that at one time in the '80s was a luxurious resort. Now, it was terribly run down and had cloudy, green water in the pool. We spent an hour and a half taking the depos, which gave us plenty of time to make our 5:00 flight.

We arrived at the airport at 2:30 without the interpreter, who was staying in Haiti for a bit to spend time with his family.

At 4:00, we learned that the flight had been cancelled. We also discovered that this was the last flight of the day heading to the US. Our minds started collectively racing, thinking of any way possible to get home to avoid spending an unexpected night in Haiti. We could have chartered a flight, but the cost was $2,000 per person, so that option was quickly eliminated.

We ended up booking the 7:00 a.m. flight back home the next morning, which meant we had an evening to spend in fabulous, downtown Port-au-Prince. American Airlines gave us transportation to a hotel along with a one-night accommodation voucher.

The three of us were driven 30 minutes to something somewhat less welcoming than the Ritz. Upon arrival, we were greeted by a staff person with a military rifle slung over his shoulder.

We checked in, and our rooms had no running water. The bed was a worn sheet covering a box spring. For dinner, we ate in the hotel restaurant. None of us could read the menu and had to order based on the pictures. I think I had a cheese sandwich, but I'm still not certain.

The next day, we put our previous day's clothes back on. We headed back to the airport and made our 7:00 flight. By 10:00 a.m., I was gratefully back on American terra firma.

Rick Levy, BA, RPR, FPR graduated from the University of Alabama in 1993 with a bachelor's degree in business management. He then enrolled in court reporting school and completed the program in 1996.

He began his reporting career with Mudrick, Witt, Levy & Consor  in Miami, Florida, and remained with them through the company sale to Esquire. He opened up his own freelance reporting firm, Network Reporting, in 2003, also in Miami.

Rick has served on the Florida Court Reporters Association Board of Directors since 2007, and he is currently the president of that organization.

Emotionally Bankrupt

By Barbara Memory, RPR, CCR

I had passed all of my final tests but one. The court reporting school only tested on Fridays, so I was interning Monday through Thursday with the firm that was going to hire me upon graduation.

One day I was in the office and an unscheduled "pop call" came in for a roundtable bankruptcy meeting. There were no reporters available.

The office manager said, "Barbara, you have to go. I have nobody else to cover this!"

I said, "No, I can't, I'm not ready. No, no, no!" And I continued to protest -- all the way down to one of the largest, oldest, and most prestigious law firms in the country. I was holding on to the promise of the office manager that I wouldn't have to read back, that there would be no transcript, that it's just a bankruptcy meeting. All I had to do was be a warm body, and write. This was in Florida, where there is no certification, so the agency was free to utilize even a lowly student!

Lo and behold, the five attorneys assembled in the conference room started arguing – at top speed, I might add. At one point, they began to simmer down, and, having forgotten the reason for the argument in the first place, turned to me to read back.

I fumbled with my notes, but was just too nervous to even see the steno. I could feel everyone staring at me. I did the next best thing to reading back: I cried.

After a few moments I composed myself, and through my tears I explained that I had not graduated yet, that I was an intern, that the agency *made* me go – but I eagerly pointed out my trusty tape recorder, and assured them that it was all on tape.

I prepared for an angry mob of lawyers to berate me, but instead, they were so kind and so nice, and they told me not to worry. They assured me that it was fine, they understood, chuckled a bit, and continued with the meeting. At its conclusion, all wished me well and good luck as I left in humiliation, still reeling from the experience.

I cried the whole way back to the reporting office. I was certain that the firm owner would be appalled and I would never get another assignment there. But she listened with compassion, even laughed. I was still devastated and did not see the humorous side. And she hired me.

I walked out of there knowing I had been given a second chance. I picked up the pieces, figured out what NOT to do next time, learned more, got better, and moved on. And today, every day, I write realtime with audiosync and have two additional awesome audio backups – just in case!

 *Barbara Memory, RPR, CCR, has been a freelance reporter since 1983. She graduated from Hillsborough College with an associate's degree in court reporting.*

She is the president and managing reporter of Memory Reporting, a freelance firm that also holds an official position with the Hon. Anthony L. Harrison in Brunswick Superior Court in Georgia. Her agency provides in-court services to Judge Harrison in five counties of South Georgia. She also sends freelance reporters to assignments throughout South Georgia and North Florida.

Barbara is a Florida Notary, as well as a certified Eclipse software trainer. She is very active in the Georgia Shorthand Reporters Association.

The Privilege of Professionalism

By Tori Pittman, BA, RPR, RDR, CRI, CVR-CM, FAPR

In this profession, you must always strive to be the best – the most ethical, the most professional, the most pleasant – because you never know who you will meet and how they may affect your future.

Case in point: Because of my past, the people I networked with, my reputation, and coupled with a little bit of synchronicity, I was able to participate in a landmark case for the country. Yes, the country.

In February of 2010, Gregory Flynt Taylor had been incarcerated for over 17 years on a murder conviction. He maintained his innocence throughout. He never once had a disciplinary report while in prison. He got several associate's degrees and worked in the jail's library.

His case was to be heard by the North Carolina Innocence Inquiry Commission on the question of his actual innocence. North Carolina is one of the first states to have developed an Innocence Inquiry Commission, whose ultimate task is to adjudicate questions of actual innocence. There are many preliminary steps that a convicted person must successfully navigate before reaching the ultimate phase, a hearing before a three-judge panel. Mr. Taylor successfully completed all prior steps and, on that February morning in 2010, came to court for his one, last shot at redemption and freedom.

Only *new* evidence is heard in these proceedings. The state of the art, or new evidence was DNA testing. In the early 1990s, the technology and science in the criminal justice system was definitely not what it is today.

After five days of testimony and argument, the panel took a day off to consider all the evidence and to discuss what they heard. Their decision *must be unanimous* in order to grant the release of the convicted person.

On the sixth day, the courtroom was packed. The TV cameras were streaming to the internet, and law students and other interested observers overflowed into the hallways.

As the judge read out the findings of fact, Greg Taylor sat in his chair at counsel table, holding counsel's hand. When the first finding of innocence was read, there was a huge eruption in the courtroom. The judge instructed all present to be quiet, because he wasn't finished reading.

After the third finding of innocence was read, pandemonium once again ensued. The District Attorney walked over and shook the now-acquitted person's hand. Mr. Taylor hugged his daughter, now an adult with a child of her own. The TV news crews and print media swarmed around the participants in this deeply moving drama, pleading for interviews. The hallway was a scene of jubilant chaos.

And I, the court reporter, was the one who took down history. I alone had the verbatim transcript of the first case in North Carolina where a panel found actual innocence.

How did I get there? By having a great reputation in the freelance arena; by developing excellent contacts over my years in reporting; by having a friend in management in the court system who kept asking me when I would come to work for him. When I finally agreed, I got the best assignment ever, working in the North Carolina Business Court, whose courtroom was located in the local law school. When the Innocence Inquiry Commission came looking for a location to hold their hearing, because I was the reporter for the courtroom with the en banc bench, I was in the right place at the right time – synchronicity – ready to take on the challenge. Most importantly, I owe my good fortune to being a professional court reporter at all times.

I will never, ever forget that experience.

Tori Pittman, BA, FAPR, RDR, CRI, CVR-CM, found the court reporting profession through the back door: by answering an ad for an office manager for a freelance agency in Raleigh, North Carolina.

In the 20 years since that fateful interview for that office manager position, she's run the office for a million-dollar agency, been a scopist, gone to court reporting school, been a freelance reporter, agency owner, CART provider, official court reporter, software trainer, and strong advocate for the court reporting profession. She is most thankful for that interview with the firm owner in 1990, because she found the career of her dreams.

Multi-Tasking: The Germany Experience

By Doreen C. Borgmann, RPR, RMR, CRR, CLVS

In the mid-90's, when I was reporting with a freelance deposition firm in New Orleans, Louisiana, my husband, a Certified Legal Video Specialist with the same firm, urged me to obtain a CLVS in order to assist him from time to time. Over the next year, I attended the requisite classes, passed the examination, and received my certification. I worked a few jobs as a CLVS, but my preference was and always has been reporting. However, one experience made the effort to achieve CLVS status worthwhile.

One day, the firm owner approached me with an offer of a job. A large ship belonging to an international shipping company had had an accident occur on board while heading up the Mississippi River toward New Orleans. The captain and crew were traveling all over the world, and the best place to depose them was at the company's headquarters in Hamburg, Germany. The client needed to schedule three days of videotaped depositions in Germany, but he only wanted to pay for one person. The question was whether I could handle both the reporting and videotaping simultaneously.

My husband and I immediately began investigating all the technical aspects that would be involved. Our first concern was electrical power. The power converter available at that time was much too heavy to carry with me. Since we were to stay at the InterContinental Hotel in Hamburg, I called the InterContinental in New Orleans, explained my problem, and inquired whether they could help me. They graciously made the arrangements for a power converter to be available at their sister hotel in Hamburg upon my arrival.

Our next problem was my ability to control both processes, reporting and videotaping, simultaneously. I obviously couldn't be both behind the camera and up close to the witness, my preferred position for reporting. Headphones with a long cord and a five-inch remote monitor and remote on/off switch enabled me to maintain my preferred position and also monitor and control my audio and video.

Our departure date arrived, and the client and I flew uneventfully to Frankfurt, where we were to connect to a flight to Hamburg. All baggage was checked except for my camera and my steno machine, which I carried on. Frankfurt, being a major hub for air traffic out of the Middle East, was particularly sensitive about security. We were required to retrieve all our baggage, go through Customs, and recheck it. Uniformed policemen armed with automatic rifles and bomb-sniffing dogs patrolled the area. At one point I was pulled out of line by a policeman and ushered to a private room, where I was questioned and my steno machine case was thoroughly examined and tested for explosives residue.

Having passed inspection, my client and I proceeded to Hamburg, which is an incredibly beautiful city with the AuBenalster (Outer Alster Lake) and Binnenalster (Inner Alster Lake) running right through the middle. The shipping company hosting the depositions was located prominently on the Binnenalster, and our hotel was on the AuBenalster. I had ample time for daytime sightseeing since our depositions were scheduled for midafternoon each day. The plaintiff's attorney was attending by telephone, and we were limited to several hours each afternoon due to the time difference.

Mechanically, everything went smoothly. All three witnesses spoke beautiful English with just a trace of accent. We had to interrupt the proceedings several times for calls to the judge back in the US to settle disputes between the contentious counsel, which I managed smoothly with my remote monitor and remote on/off switch.

When all the depositions were completed, my client and I found a beer garden along the shores of the lake, where we sampled several of the wonderful local German beers and watched the sailboats and sculling races for the rest of the daylight hours.

Our trip home, however, was a disaster! At the Frankfurt airport, my client was obsessed with the duty-free shop. I made a couple of small purchases and then waited for him outside, frequently admonishing him to hurry. When we finally made it to the counter, our seats had been given away. We managed to get on the next flight, but we were routed through Cincinnati with no guaranteed connection into New Orleans. In Cincinnati, he was able to get only one seat going to New Orleans, which I urged him to take since he was going home to small children. I waited several hours before getting a flight for home.

In spite of the potential drawbacks to traveling to and in foreign countries, I had a glorious experience and would do it again in a heartbeat.

Doreen C. Borgmann, RMR, CRR, CLVS, was born in Detroit, Michigan and grew up in rural central Mississippi. After college, she worked in New Orleans, Louisiana, as a legal secretary for eight years before meeting and marrying her husband, Richard, in

1974. They moved to Los Angeles, California, where she attended Bryan College of Court Reporting and obtained her California CSR in 1975. She reported in the Los Angeles area until 1986, when she moved back to Mississippi, where she reported as an official for six years, then moved back to New Orleans and, eventually, to Phoenix, Arizona, her husband's home town, in 2001, where she is a freelance reporter.

She has served as an officer for the Los Angeles General Court Reporters Association and the California Court Reporters Association for many years, and is presently serving as immediate past president of the Arizona Court Reporters Association.

• • •

Vignette 2: The Measure of a Man

By Gene Lee, CSR-TX

It's hard to choose just a few things that I have encountered over 35 years. Most of my years I worked neither in a high-profile court nor in one that is located in a large city, so the reader would think I've led a boring existence out in the boonies. On the contrary; I have witnessed things I would never have seen in more urban environments.

An unpleasant case, to say the least, the sexual assault of a child, brought a quick reaction by my judge and the jury when the defendant was testifying. His defense was that he could not be guilty of the crime because his organ was too large to penetrate the little girl.

Once the defendant made that statement on the witness stand, his attorney followed up with the question, "How big is it?"

Half the jurors started groaning, and the judge intervened. "Now, hold on here, Counsel. You've gone too far. Ladies and gentlemen, please retire to the jury room."

Before the jurors had a chance to get up and follow the judge's instruction, the defendant addressed the court directly: "Judge, I wasn't going to whip it out. I was just going to use my fingers to show how big around it is."

After an awkward few seconds of silence, the judge ordered the jurors to remain in the jury box, and the testimony continued.

The defendant was found guilty. I don't think he did himself any favors with that testimony.

Gene Lee, Texas CSR, has reported for 35 years in Austin, New Orleans, Miami, and Dallas, with the last 28 of those years as the 22nd State District court reporter for a tri-county district just south of Austin, Texas.

Over the years, he has served on many committees in his state association, written articles for both the Journal of Court Reporting and the Texas Record, and given a speech at the National Court Reporters Association convention in San Diego, California.

He is the second in line of four siblings, all of whom are court reporters, and he was the first to realize what a great profession it is. His wife, Brenda, has been his scopist for 19 years.

I'm Late, I'm Late, for a Very Important Date...

By Marlene "Hedy" Coleman, RPR, RMR, CRR

When the telephone's three rings roused me from a deep sleep, fear, dread and panic greeted me with the morning light. I turned to my nemesis, a silent analog clock face whose large hand pointed to the 9 and the small hand on the 10, before picking up the receiver. I felt the noose around my neck as I choked out a hello.

"Hedy, where are you?" Judge Smith's secretary demanded. "The jurors are in the box and the judge is getting ready to take the bench. What should I tell him?"

"Tell him I died."

Ann, my supervisor, sounded panicked and desperate as she asked, "Seriously, what can I say?"

"Ann," I croaked, "I overslept. Either my alarm went off and I didn't hear it, or it doesn't work anymore." Either way, I was done for.

"I would cover for you," Ann said, "but you have to read back to the jury today. They want you to repeat the medical examiner's testimony *and* his report."

Then I remembered that I had planned to come in early that morning and scan my notes before reading them to the jury. Now I have to read the ME's testimony cold! My imagination ran wild. The judge will embarrass me and taunt me in front of the jury before he hands me my walking papers, I'm sure.

"I am out the door, Ann. Please light candles, pray to the gods, and do voodoo dances for me!"

I dressed quickly and hoped that the car keys were where I thought I had left them the night before. I wasn't sure whether I had locked the front door as I sped off, but having the house ransacked by burglars hiding in the bushes (maybe they got in last night, were hiding, and I could blame *them* for turning my alarm off) was not a concern at the moment.

Our courtrooms were "temporary" buildings that were still designated "temporary" 15 years later. They were perched on a hillside, and parking was at the bottom, so of course, I had to run up the hill, struggling to maintain a semblance of professionalism.

I don't know whether the courtroom clock was smiling or smirking, because I had made it in just over 30 minutes. Perspiration cascaded down my back in a sticky waterfall. I was a mess.

The judge's secretary showed empathy bordering on pity when I asked her if I could speak with him privately. "You can try," she said doubtfully.

I hesitated at the door as if waiting for divine intervention to give me the words to talk my way out of this. My timid knock, and slow, gentle opening of the door, didn't soften the glacial glance that met mine. I decided it was best to speak first.

"Your Honor, I apologize for being late, and I assure you, it will never happen again." I tried to think of something clever or humorously self-deprecating to say, but nothing was forthcoming. I wasn't sure whether the judge was even listening to me. He busied himself with the paperwork on his desk in a way that signaled to me that this encounter was briskly coming to a close. I beat a hasty retreat out of his office and went down the hall toward the courtroom.

Thirty seconds later, I noticed the judge further down the hallway, preparing to assume the bench. I kept my fingers crossed and sent up another silent prayer as I entered the courtroom and took my place. The jurors' glare told me they were not happy about waiting for the reporter for almost 45 minutes.

I nervously sorted through my notes — it was precomputer days, folks! — trying to locate the appropriate pile, all the while making deals with the gods. Finally – hallelujah – my hands grasped the correct folds of testimony like a lover returning from the battlefield.

After the bailiff boomed his call to order, the spectre of a potential nightmare really began for me. I was going to read back a thick stack of cold notes!

Thank goodness my years of court reporter training and experience in handling struggles, enduring stresses, and surviving strains paid off. My notes were pearls that would have impressed any perfectionist reporter (certainly a redundant term), and I read fluidly and without hesitation. With the jury satisfied and admonished, they retired to further deliberate, and I set off to formally beg forgiveness from my superior.

Ann was extremely gracious and kind. She chuckled as she recommended I invest in two good alarm clocks, and use them both religiously.

Later that day, the jury returned a verdict. I packed up my equipment and my notes and, as was my custom, extended my appreciation to the clerk and the secretary. The latter whispered urgently that if I wanted to keep my job, I had better go in to the judge and grovel for a second time.

My knock at the door was little less timid than before, as I felt good about the reading I had just completed. The judge actually greeted me cordially this time. Memories of my Catholic school days flooded back. I felt just like I did when I was summoned to "the parlour," a place that was normally off limits to mere mortals unless we were being banished, suspended or facing the wrath of God for some sin we had unwittingly committed.

"What can I do for you, Hedy?" My mind snapped back to the present. I tried to muster enough confidence to project a fearless demeanor and began my apology anew.

"I am so sorry for my lateness." The judge interrupted me with a wave of his hand, hardly looking up. "Oh, that's fine. Don't worry about it."

In the uncomfortable silence, I inched toward the door, wanting and needing to leave while I still had a job.

"Can we talk?" he said quietly.

I froze. I couldn't tell whether his Honor was about to divulge national secrets or he was going to recruit me to spy on others in the judiciary.

He leaned forward on his elbows. "Hedy, could you tell me why the reporters are scared of me? Maybe you can shed some light on this, perhaps give me some advice."

How was I going to reveal that he has a rotten reputation in the personnel relations arena; that he has been known to fire reporters at the drop of a pack of paper; that he is loudly intolerant of even a rare poor readback; and he is feared by virtually everyone connected to the legal system of the county – how could I do all that and still keep the job I nearly lost just minutes before?

My reply surprised even me. With a concerned, serious tilt of my head, I answered, "Well, Judge, you don't smile very much."

He chuckled – just like a real human – then inquired, "Oh, really? You think that's it?"

"Yes, I think so," I replied, my voice oozing sincerity.

He heartily thanked me for being honest, and I floated out, having survived another day with the man. To everyone's surprise and disbelief, from that point on, although Judge Smith's reputation remained that of a tough justice, in his dealings with court personnel, his personality morphed into that of a considerate, caring individual, complete with glowing smile.

What a win-win: a happy reporter (who still has a job), and a happy jurist (who still has a happy reporter)!

Marlene "Hedy" Coleman, RPR, CMR, CRR was born and raised in Honolulu, Hawaii. She attended Bryan College of Court Reporting in Los Angeles, California. She is licensed in both California and Hawaii, and currently works as a freelance reporter in Honolulu.

Vignette 3: Maybe Just One Little White Lie...

By Jacqueline M. Timmons, RPR, RMR, RDR, CSR, FAPR

In my 30 years of reporting, I would like to think that I have seen just about everything, but that is never the case. When you work in a career where the players frequently change from day to day, and often the cases and circumstances change as well, one must be prepared for anything.

When I lived in Florida as a new reporter, I went on a deposition in a criminal case and gave the oath to the witness, inquiring whether he swears/affirms to tell the truth. The assumed response is, "I do."

Never assume.

The witness said, *"I don't."*

At first I thought I misheard, but before I had a chance to say or do anything, the lawyer asked the witness if he just said he was not going to tell the truth. The witness confirmed, yes, that is indeed what he said, and the deposition was canceled. That truly was a new one on me.

Jacqueline M. Timmons, CSR, RDR, FAPR, is a 1979 graduate of Southern Illinois University at Carbondale with an Associate's Degree in court reporting. She worked as a freelance reporter in Miami, Florida, from June of 1981 to February of 1986 and in Chicago, Illinois, from February 1986 to present. In addition to reporting depositions and doing court work, she specializes in convention reporting.

Growing up in Rockford, Illinois, she was able to write Gregg shorthand at 160 wpm, and her high school guidance counselor suggested court reporting.

Jackie has served the Illinois State Court Reporting Association in several capacities, including Northern Regional representative, secretary, vice president, president and immediate past president. She has also served on National Court Reporters Association committees, most recently as Chair of the Membership Telemarketing Committee and also as a member of the National Court Reporters Foundation Angels Committee.

When she is not reporting, Jackie enjoys crafts of all types. An experienced and avid knitter, she creates "chemo hats" to be worn by those undergoing cancer treatment, delivering these gifts to patients right at the hospital where her brother had once received therapy for the disease. She also makes them for friends and family afflicted by the illness.

Live Auction Surprise

By Theresa Marie (Tess) Crowder, RPR, CRR, CBC, CCP

The First Annual Black Tie Gala, a fundraiser for the local Deaf Service Center, was scheduled to begin at 7:00 p.m. I entered the ballroom at 5:00, and my stress level was in the high range as I set up my equipment and then anxiously tracked down someone, anyone, for the information needed for my dictionary, which I had been requesting for weeks prior to the event.

Fresh off the press, I grabbed the printed program to search for proper names, corporate sponsors, a list of speakers, and the agenda for the evening. As I was frantically preparing my job dictionary, a kind employee/server of the facility offered me a beverage from the open bar. Although it was tempting, I reluctantly declined.

As the crowd began to pour in through the double doors, I was nearing the end of the program booklet in preparation for the ceremonies. All that was remaining in the booklet was a list of items to be auctioned. I asked the program chair, who was a close friend of mine and late-deafened, if this information of auction items would be necessary for my preparation work. She signed to me the welcoming news that the information on these pages would not be needed. I was thankful that this event included a *silent* auction; how appropriate, was my thought, for a Deaf event.

After the opening remarks were concluded, we were all seated for a five-course meal. I felt honored to be sitting at the table with the master of ceremonies, a local celebrity and well-respected member of our community. After introducing myself and explaining my role in this event, I half-jokingly asked if he would be speaking slowly and clearly for me. The laughter that erupted following this question had me wondering if he misunderstood or even heard my words. Not until after the fact did I understand his wholehearted chuckle.

The speakers, skits, and speeches following the meal went well. As they were announcing the information for the winners of the silent auction, I released a quiet sigh of relief, confident that we were wrapping up the evening. As the remarks were drawing to a close, the emcee announced, "We are now ready to begin the live auction!"

WHAT?!?! The *LIVE* auction?!? I thought this was supposed to be a *SILENT* auction!! This is every captioner's worst nightmare! I was told I didn't need to prepare for this list of items from the program book! How can I possibly CART an auctioneer? My eyes must have looked like saucers as my back stiffened and my jaw dropped. My vision shot towards my friend sitting at her table across the room. As I got her attention, I quickly signed to her my comments of disbelief and horror. She broke into laughter as she was signing, "I'm sorry! I'm sorry!"

As I'm sure many captioners and CART providers have experienced, I instantly switched into adrenalin mode, typing at speeds I had only ever dreamed of before this night. This is a great example of why we need excellent fingerspelling skills, spelling names of people who donated the items, the brand names of these items, the companies with which they are associated, the names of the celebrities and artists who had autographed these items, etc. And numbers, numbers, numbers. Fortunately, auctioneers repeat themselves many times during the bidding process, my saving grace. I now understood the meaning of that chuckle from the emcee about speaking "slowly and clearly."

By the end of the evening, I was more than ready for that cocktail that had been offered to me prior to the gala. Unfortunately, the open bar was now a closed bar, so I would have to wait until I arrived at the comfort and safety of my home to enjoy a glass of red wine. As I was struggling to calm my nerves, recounting the challenges of the evening, I forced myself to focus on the kind words expressed by the attendees who were so thankful and appreciative of the CART services I had provided that evening.

I have just participated in my seventh Annual Black Tie Gala, proud to be able to say I have successfully CARTed an auctioneer once again. I met up with the same emcee this year, who also has participated for the last seven years, and we still share a laugh about that first night, seven years ago, when I was baptized with my first live auction.

Theresa Marie (Tess) Crowder , RPR, CRR, CBC, CCP is president of Realtime Communication Services, Inc. She is on the boards of the Clearwater chapter of the Hearing Loss Association, the Suncoast chapter of the Association of Late-Deafened Adults, and Blossom Montessori School for the Deaf.

She has been providing CART services for the Deaf, Late Deaf, and Hard-of-Hearing communities since 1995. Tess conducts seminars instructing CART providers and captioners on sensitivity issues and basic conversational signing, and has presented workshops about CART services for local, state, and national organizations.

She has established a new non-profit organization named Communication Access, Inc., which provides services for people with hearing loss, and is a longtime volunteer with the Association of Late-Deafened Adults and local Hearing Loss Association of America chapters. Tess volunteers CART services for mental health and rehabilitation counseling sessions; for workshops, meetings, and conventions for non-profits; and teaches children and adults basic conversational sign language. She is also a contributing editor of the National Court Reporters Association's Journal of Court Reporting.

The Rain in Spain Falls Mainly in Bahrain

By Deanna P. Baker, RPR, RMR, FAPR

It was difficult to think of one certain scenario in my 30-year career as a court reporter, CART provider, and now captioner, especially when my first officialship started out working for the judge I appeared *before* just three years earlier *in juvenile court*!

I think my fondest and funniest adventure was in the early 1990s, when I was assigned to cover depositions taking place in Cairo, Kuwait, Jordan and Bahrain. It was a highly technical case that I had been working on for quite a few months

We had a ton of equipment with us, including my Toshiba "laptop" (with the lovely amber screen) that weighed more than my steno machine and case, and the bulky wheelies that we used back then. I made it a practice to always keep my passport in plain sight. In fact, my passport came away from this trip with my teeth marks in it.

After what seemed like days in the air, getting through immigration, dealing with crowds everywhere including herds of sheep crossing the streets, we finally arrived at the hotel in Cairo, not knowing what day it was. I found out that the attorneys booked the group of us on the executive level of the hotel, which was very nice. I was excited to see that my room faced the Nile River – until I opened my window. The stench of the river and the car exhaust was overwhelming, as was the incessant horn honking.

We had an extra day before depositions to regroup, catch up on sleep and do a little sightseeing. The next morning we headed out for one of many days of depositions. My computer was really for my own use in getting as quick a turnaround as possible, but it was quickly learned that the deponents' grasp of the English language was better when they could read the questions.

After each day, I was doing my best to get rough drafts finished, and being that this was before the era of internet-everything, I needed to find something that resembled Fed Ex to mail my 5-½-inch floppy disk back to my scopist. I quickly learned that a female is pretty much ignored here unless a gentleman accompanies her, so my trusty lawyers helped out and got me what I needed. They also were very helpful when I blew fuses many times in my room plugging in my Baron TX, even though I was using all the right protectors. Thankfully the TX wasn't harmed, just the hotel's electric connection.

The attorneys invited me to a business dinner with the clients, as they knew I couldn't get served in the hotel restaurant without one of them there. The client was a fairly high-profile man who traveled with many armed bodyguards. It was delightful to listen to him talk about his country, its customs, the food we were eating; yet the entire time, two men with large weapons were seated behind him. Needless to say, that put a damper on my appetite. I was instructed not to ask him any questions. I had had a briefing ahead of time that I wasn't to speak unless spoken to, which was actually fine by me.

After a few days in Cairo, we moved on to Kuwait. It was a much shorter flight, thankfully, as sitting next to a man clutching an assault rifle was very unsettling. To make matters worse, he was smoking a horrible cigar that nearly put me under.

As we checked into the Kuwaiti hotel, I noticed the scorched marble of the floor, left over from the bombings and the oil fires of the Gulf War. In addition, we were issued stern warnings from the hotel staff not to step in dirt or sand, as they hadn't found all the grenades yet.

The next day we only had one deposition scheduled, and our driver was more than happy to show us around the city. The Gulf War had ended just a short time before our arrival, and many buildings were in shambles. Five times a day we heard the call to prayer, audible from anywhere in the city, an eerie sound for this Midwestern girl.

Our last scheduled trip was to Bahrain, again, another short flight, although the pilot had to navigate around a no-fly zone in the course of the trip. We were only scheduled there for one night, which is a shame, as the buildings were glorious. Everything was meticulous, and so much was gold-plated.

We arrived very late in the evening to an amazing hotel, and an extravagant party was just getting started in the lounge. I was exhausted, and went straight to my room. I turned on the TV, not sure what I was going to find, and to my amazement, *The Rocky Horror Picture Show* was playing! No wonder they think Americans are strange.

With the deposition concluded in Bahrain, it happened that we needed one last witness who was in Jordan – again, another short flight. Again, I boarded the plane with passport in teeth.

We were fortunate to arrive at another beautiful location, with an elegant hotel. Since the witness wasn't very cooperative, we ended up waiting a full day before the deposition started. I finally had time to lounge by a pool – the size of Cleveland!

Once that mission was accomplished, our journey home was underway. It was such a rich experience, some good, some bad; but it certainly makes coming home all the more meaningful.

Deanna P. Baker, RPR, RMR, FAPR, graduated from the American Institute of Commerce in Iowa in 1981. She reported in the Quad City area until 1983 when she moved to Seattle.

While in Washington State, she was an official for four years, owned her own freelance agency and worked with Larsen & Smith. Deanna held various offices in the Washington Shorthand Reporters Association including president from 1992-1993.

In 1994 Deanna moved to Tucson and provided CART services at

the University of Arizona, as well as continued her freelance captioning work. In 1999 she was appointed to the Tucson Commission on Disability Issues.

Deanna was chair of the NCRA Captioning Task Force and in 2004 was appointed to the NCRA Captioning Community of Interest, being named Chair the following year.

Currently, she is a freelance realtime captioner/consultant residing in Flagstaff, Arizona.

Vignette 4: Th-Th-Th-That's All, Folks!

By Joseph O. Inquagiato, RPR, RMR, CSR

In the early stages of your career, it doesn't take long to realize that reporting out in the field is nothing like taking down carefully measured in-school dictation. Witnesses mutter, trail off, and speak with hands covering their mouths. Stopping the proceedings even for a few seconds to ask that something be repeated seems like the worst thing imaginable to the neophyte reporter.

In an early criminal trial I reported, the crucial witness – the victim of the crime – spoke with a stutter. Although nervous, I was determined to get through the proceeding without interrupting. It was difficult, but I hung on to the introductory questions and answers, convincing myself it would be smooth sailing ahead.

Then the increasingly nervous witness was asked to provide a narrative involving the events leading to the criminal charges – a crucial part of the trial. It seemed that he began to speak *very* fast, and I realized I couldn't understand him at all. I had no choice but to interrupt and ask him to repeat his answer more slowly so I could make an accurate record.

The witness looked me square in the eye, and in a loud voice, with no trace of a stutter, proclaimed, "I ain't *said* nothing yet!" Needless to say, judge and courtroom burst into laughter, while I sat there mortified.

I like to share this story with students for a very specific reason: With the advent of steno machines that record audio, many new reporters feel they will never need to interrupt a proceeding. However, as this story demonstrates, if you can't understand something the first time, never assume that listening to the audio afterward is going to make it any clearer. Audio can be a helpful tool, but it will never replace a court reporter. It is your responsibility to make certain proceedings are both heard and understood – even if it leaves you with a red face.

Joseph O. Inquagiato, RPR, RMR, CSR, has been a working reporter since 1962 in the State of New York. He was an official reporter in the 7th Judicial District for 20 years, and the owner of Alliance Shorthand Reporters, Inc., from 1978 through 2006.

Joseph served as President of the New York State Shorthand Reporters Association in the early 1970s, was elected as a Fellow of the Academy of Professional Reporters in 1985, and was nominated and selected as a finalist for the 2000 Nathaniel Award in Rochester, New York, in recognition of his "exceptional dedication to the legal profession, going above and beyond the call of duty. "

In his retirement, he continues to act as advisor and mentor to court reporting students.

A Closet Reporter

By Richard Bursky, BA, RPR, RMR, CRR, CCR

"Did you do something wrong? Why is the FBI asking about you?" My next-door neighbor greeted me with these queries, and she was more than a little interested in my response. The FBI investigation into my private life was the prelude to one of the most unusual cases I have ever reported.

While I was an official federal reporter in the US District Court for the Southern District of New York, my chief reporter suggested that since I already had a fairly high-level FBI security clearance to work in the Grand Jury, I would be the best candidate to quickly and seamlessly attain the top-secret designation the feds were seeking for all essential personnel connected with a very sensitive case just filed in our court. It piqued my interest, and I readily agreed.

What ensued was a mountain of paperwork I had to spend hours filling out. It called for information reaching back to my elementary school days. I amazed myself that I was able to recall the names of my first through sixth grade teachers. Oddly enough, I didn't do as well naming my junior high and high school instructors!

After the necessary documents were submitted, I was informed that various family members, friends, neighbors, and colleagues would be interviewed; hence, the curious and concerned questions, as mentioned before, as well as phone calls from friends and family around the country wondering what was up. I even heard from an old college roommate living and working in Israel who was contacted.

I was informed that I had successfully passed muster, my college hippie days notwithstanding, and the government seemed satisfied with my level of patriotism and character. I was then summoned to the US Attorney's office to be briefed on the case. It had turned out that federal agents discovered and captured a spy whose day job was that of a professor at a local university.

The government attorney in charge explained that this case was so sensitive, that all the pretrial hearings needed to be conducted in an ultra-secure location where there was no chance that any listening device could capture the content of the proceedings. The only place that the FBI and the US Attorney's office could use that met those parameters in the downtown New York City area was a four-foot-by-six-foot storage closet at the Bureau's offices in the then-standing World Trade Center. The location was acceptable particularly because the walls of the closet were lined with two feet of lead, making surreptitious recording virtually impossible.

Once or twice a week for the next three months, the Closet Courtroom assembled at the designated spot. The judge convened the proceedings with the Assistant United States Attorney, defense counsel, occasionally the defendant, and myself. I was seated on a little stool in front of my steno machine, while all the others stood around me, creating a sort of tight legal sandwich, elbow-to-elbow, as motions were argued and rulings made.

As these secret hearings in this case dwindled, there came a point where I heard nothing about it for nearly a month. I ran into the Assistant US Attorney assigned to the case in the halls of the courthouse, and he mentioned that the case had basically gone away. One of *our* spies had been captured in another country, and the accused had been traded for that American agent's freedom.

I have since reported proceedings on a park bench, on a super-freighter docked at the pier, in Don Shula's office at his country club; but reporting a spy case in a lead-lined FBI closet has been by far the most unusual venue of my reporting career.

Richard Bursky, BA, RPR, RMR, CRR, CCR, began his career in 1974 as a New York City freelance reporter with Fink & Carney Reporting, moving on to an officialship at the United States District Court for the Southern District in Manhattan, serving four of his eight years there as deputy chief reporter. He has also freelanced in Florida, and presently resides in Atlanta, Georgia working as an independent contractor.

Richard is on the advisory board of the Brown College of Court Reporting, and mentors newly graduating students. He is also a certified performance life coach. He has enjoyed working with English bulldog rescue for many years, and is on the board of Casey's Kids, a non-profit organization whose goal is to supply students in underserved communities with the tools they need to succeed.

The Pen Is Mightier than the Valentine

By Donald J. White, RPR, RMR, CSR

Part of the commercial course of study I took was Gregg shorthand and typing. My first steno class was as one of the few males in a predominantly female student population.

In the first month of Gregg I, it was customary to read aloud one sentence per student from our shorthand book. We did so going around the room in an orderly fashion so that everyone would have a turn. One bright, sunny day in class, as usual, I figured out by mentally matching the sentences to the number of students ahead of me, and silently practiced the passage that I was meant to read back.

Unfortunately, math was never my strong suit, and I realized just seconds before the moment of my turn that I had miscalculated. The passage I was to read was something I had not even glanced at, much less practiced.

Much of the genius of Gregg writing depends on the proportion of the stroke outlines, i.e., the letter "e" is a small circle, while the letter "a" is slightly larger; "n" is a short, flat stroke, and the "m" is slightly larger.

The sentence that I was to enunciate was, "Mary had an enemy." I was so distracted by my full-blown anxiety, I did not concentrate on the strokes that lay on the paper clearly before me. To my horror, I heard myself blurt out, "Mary had an *enema.*"

The class divided into one group of shocked gasps; one more gregarious group of catcalls and boos; and a third of classic Bronx cheers and Brooklyn chaos; all leaving me a red-faced, flop-sweated kid.

The teacher dragged me out by my ear from the class into the hallway. She informed me that, as a result of my unacceptable behavior, I would not, no matter what skill I achieve in the class, receive a passing grade. Sure enough, even though I excelled in both Gregg and typing, she failed me, and I was forced to repeat the course.

The next term I had a male teacher, jazz head, alto sax player, and since I was also a fledgling drummer, we hit it off right away. I knew this semester was going to be a good, one; I just didn't know how good.

Like Charlie Brown, I had admired a beautiful "red-haired girl" from afar for quite some time, but could never work up the courage to speak to her. It turned out in the new semester she was in my Gregg I class. Having done this before, I knew my way around the syllabus, and she thought I was *really* talented in shorthand skills.

We'll be celebrating 55 years of marriage this fall. In part, I owe my everlasting good fortune to that old, cranky teacher, who made it all possible. So there you are. If I had no further connection with shorthand, my life would be fantastic, having the best life partner in the world.

 *Donald J. White, RPR, RMR, CSR (Retired), graduated from Interboro Institute in New York City, first using Gregg shorthand and later the steno machine as his tools of choice in his career. In the US Army, he worked in Inchon, Korea as a courts-martial reporter.*

He worked for the Unemployment Insurance office as a hearing reporter, and served as chief Grand Jury reporter of Nassau County, New York. He later accepted an official position with the reporters' office at the United States District Court for the Southern District of New York, where he was chief reporter for one year.

Don was elected to the Federation of Shorthand Reporters, a freelance organization, as secretary-treasurer. He also served a term as president of the New York State Court Reporters Association from 1981 to 1983.

Don qualified in the 1979 PASCRA speed contest, and walked away with first place in the 1980 NYSCRA speed competition.

Fists of Fury

By Thomas J. Kresse, RPR

The court reporting profession has taken me on many adventures around the world, and given me an incredible education, not to mention innumerable stories. This is one I can actually tell you about:

In the winter of 1978-1979, before launching my own firm, I was given an assignment to report the deposition of an illegal immigrant detainee in custody at the Miami-Dade County stockade. He was a young Colombian man about to be deported to his home country.

He was also the lover of an older woman involved in a will contest in Probate Court. In fact, his former lover wanted him deported so that he could not testify against her in the probate matter, and she was the one responsible for turning him in to the authorities. For purposes of this recounting, I'll call her Sarah, and the young man will be Enrique.

I met my client, Mr. Smith, at the entrance to the detention facility. As we waited to be admitted, he instructed me to report any and every word uttered during the deposition, repeating and reemphasizing, *"any and every word."*

In the deposition room were myself; Mr. Smith; Enrique, the very nervous and frightened witness, who, by the way, spoke no English; Sarah, the witness' former lover who was the main party in the will contest; her attorney, Mr. Jones; and the interpreter. We also had a deputy standing guard just outside the door.

Needless to say, it was a very heated examination, with emotions running wild. During the proceeding, Sarah would sardonically smile at Enrique while slowly and quietly with her index finger executing a slicing motion across her throat.

My client, upon noticing this gesture, put a descriptive statement of Sarah's actions on the record. Her attorney, Mr. Jones, gruffly turned to me and commanded, "Off the record," and then began to curse out Mr. Smith, Enrique, even his own client, *and* the interpreter! This scene played out three times during the deposition, and I, true to my previous instructions, each time noted the command to go off the record as well as the ensuing obscenities.

In the midst of a fourth tirade of expletives (not deleted) following the "off the record" statement, Mr. Jones suddenly noticed that I was still pounding the keys, faithfully reporting his comments. He screamed at me, "You were told to go off the record!"

I calmly informed him of my earlier instructions, noting that agreement had to be reached between counsel in order to go off the record, and there was no such accord. In disbelief, he bellowed a question, "So were you recording all my earlier statements too?" to which I replied in the affirmative.

At this point, Jones lunged across the table that separated us, attempting to grab the paper notes out of my tray. Reflexively, I pushed my chair straight back. I was prevented, fortunately, from toppling over backwards by the wall close behind me.

Grasping my steno machine firmly between my legs, feet up off the floor and chair angled against the wall, I continued to write. Smith, my client, grabbed the arms of the charging attorney who was now sprawled across the table and within inches of the paper tray. Jones threw the first punch at Smith, and the two jumped headlong into a good, old-fashioned slugfest, with me literally between and under the pugilists, desperately trying to protect myself and my equipment from the punches and kicks.

So much for filing this as a *civil* matter.

The deputy came to the rescue, separating the two and threatening both of them with arrest and lockup in the adjoining room. I emerged unscathed, machine intact, notes still fully in my possession.

I don't remember what happened to the attorneys, the parties, or what the resolution of the case was, but true to my professionalism, all participants received a *clean* transcript of the proceedings, literally and figuratively: verbatim testimony, obscenity-laced colloquy, all of it — *sans* the bloodstains on my steno notes.

Tom Kresse, RPR, became a freelance court reporter in the early 1970s, worked a year in New York City, moved to Miami, Florida in 1975, and hung out his own shingle as Thomas J. Kresse & Associates in 1980.

Give Her a Hand

By Maxyne G. Bursky, BA, RPR, CRR, CCR

Assigned for 2:00 p.m., the Workers' Compensation deposition appeared on its face to be a ho-hum, one-hour interruption of my shopping day. There were the usual suspects, Janie Jones, claimant, versus Confidential Communications Service, Inc., employer, and the company's insurer/carrier.

The woman bringing the action was sworn, and I settled in to report "left hand/right hand," a euphemism I use to describe a very simple, no-brainer proceeding. She was 43, and worked out of her home, one of 10 to 15 such employees in her position. She was being treated for wrist and elbow pain, and had had to have an operation to relieve the symptoms. But the company was not paying for it.

The first clue that I had that this was not going to be the vanilla deposition I assumed, was the manner in which the following questions were answered:

> Q.   *What was your job title at CCS?*
> A.   *Tele-passion consultant.*
> Q.   *What job duties did you have?*
> A.   *I had oral sex with clients over the phone.*
> Q.   *You mean phone sex?*
> A.   *Exactly.*

It seemed that Janie had quite a following, and she was busy at her job several hours each day. Having to hold the phone in one hand, usually with her elbow perched on the kitchen table, had become quite a chore, and led to the constant pain and subsequent corrective surgery.

I couldn't help recalling those 1-900 number commercials that would air on TV at 2:00 a.m. between episodes of *I Love Lucy*. The actors in those advertisements looked to me to be twentysomething porn star wannabes. Janie was way outside of that weight class, and the brown/gray roots of her hair beat her dyed blonde portion by at least three inches.

This was no vanilla depo; this one was chock full o' nuts.

Priorities

By Rick Levy, BBA, RPR

As both an avid golfer and court reporter, I was more than excited to get the assignment to take the deposition of the greatest golfer to ever live – Jack Nicklaus. I have also taken Tiger Woods' depo, but meeting Nicklaus was the ultimate privilege.

The examination was to commence at 10:00 a.m. in Mr. Nicklaus' lawyer's office in Palm Beach, Florida. It was a case I had worked on before, and I was really looking forward to meeting "The Bear." The proceeding was expected to take no more than two hours, but I still saw no problem traveling the hour-plus it would take me to drive to the location. Present in the conference room were two named partner attorneys representing the plaintiff; one managing partner appearing on behalf of the defendant; a senior partner of yet another law firm for an insurance company; the witness and his personal/business attorney; and myself and the videographer. We began at ten sharp; no small wonder, considering the legal meters that were simultaneously running in that room.

At 10:45 there was a knock on the door from a secretary who handed Mr. Nicklaus a sticky note which read, "Call your wife immediately." Everything stopped, of course, to allow him to determine the nature of the emergency. The golf champion reentered the room and announced that his wife needed him home because the curtain people were at the house, and she needed his help with the selection of the fabrics and style.

The attorneys decided that this would be a good time for a (very early) lunch recess. Mr. Nicklaus promised to return at noon. At 1:00 p.m., the proceedings resumed, ending about 2:00 p.m. Total on the record, under two hours; total time, including travel, more than six hours. On parting, Mr. Nicklaus mentioned that a few weeks earlier, he left a business meeting to attend Grandparents Day at his grandchild's elementary school. This is a pretty classy guy who has his priorities straight.

A Trial of Tragedy

By William Cohen, RPR, RMR, FAPR

One morning in the middle of June, I received a telephone call from my boss: "Bill, this is Julian. I know it's nearing the end of June and you're looking forward to a well-deserved vacation, but Judge Smith, a judge in an outlying district, was indicted some time ago for the crime of subornation of perjury, and removed from the bench pending the outcome of his criminal trial, which is now scheduled to start on July 6 and which will last six weeks.

"They're trying this case during vacation time in order not to clog the fall court calendar. The other local judges have recused themselves, so they're sending in an out-of-town judge to preside. As Chief Court Reporter of our judicial district, I've been contacted to personally handle the reporting chores. So in addition to assigning myself to this lucrative job, I'd like you to join me."

"I'd be more than happy to," I quickly replied, daily-copy dollar bills dancing before my eyes. "What exactly was the crime, Julian?"

"Apparently, before he was elected judge a couple of years ago, he was the attorney representing a local real estate developer. The previous year, the State Legislature passed a law that when land was purchased for the purpose of development, the owners would not be permitted to "flip" it, that is, purchase the land and then sell it virtually the next day, usually at a handsome profit. The developers had to make an affidavit promising to actually build on the plot.

"His client bought a 40-acre tract and did in fact make an affidavit in which he promised not to flip it. He promised, as required by law, to develop it, and the affidavit was signed by his attorney, Mr. Smith. The Special Prosecutor in the case alleged that Judge Smith, the developer's attorney at the time, knew the affidavit was false, knew that his client was intending to flip and not build on the property. So Judge Smith was indicted for subornation of perjury of his client, that is, knowingly obtaining false testimony."

The trial began promptly on July 6 to great publicity in the local press, and ended on August 19 with a jury verdict of guilty. The defendant appealed the guilty verdict to the Appellate Division. The appellate judges not only reversed the verdict, but threw out the indictment altogether, opining that since the injunction against flipping appeared only in the preface of the statute and not in its body, the flipping aspect was construed to not be part of the law; and since perjury by definition is swearing falsely to a *material* fact, the flipping was immaterial since it was prefatory. Therefore, there being no perjury, there cannot be subornation of perjury.

While this was seemingly, in my lay view, a strained legalistic interpretation, the defendant was, of course, overjoyed. He requested that the Appellate Division immediately reinstate him to his judgeship.

The Appellate Division said no, reasoning that, during the course of the trial, Smith had taken the witness stand and testified that he had notarized the affidavit by having his client mail the signed affidavit to him. Smith had then executed the jurat several days later outside the presence of the affiant.

New York Notary Public law requires that the signature of an affiant *must* be taken in the affiant's presence. Therefore, according to the defendant (and his defense), it was not a valid affidavit. The Appellate Division said that since Smith had, out of his own mouth, testified to a violation of the Notary Public law, he was unfit to sit as a judge, although he could continue to practice law.

This ruling so upset the former judge that, while he tried to return to his law firm, he could not reconcile himself to his brilliant career having been shattered so ignominiously. He began to drink to the point of becoming an alcoholic. Two years after the Appellate Division ruling, his wife divorced him. He subsequently committed suicide.

William Cohen, RPR, RMR, FAPR, has been reporting for more than half a century. He is a familiar figure at the National Court Reporters Association meetings and conventions, and is a member of the National Court Reporters Foundation Angels.

In World War II, he and his brother, sergeants in the Army Air Corps, became court reporters for the Judge Advocate General's office. After the war, they served as court reporters for war crimes trials in the Philippines.

The Cohen brothers won the NCRA speed contests given in the 1950s six times, collectively. In 1969, Bill was recognized with the NCRA Distinguished Service Award.

Bill worked for many years as an official reporter for the United States District Court for the Southern District of New York in Manhattan. He presently freelances with Chelsea Reporting in New York City.

Vignette 5: BO-WAU-SUH

By Gene Lee, CSR-TX

In just my second year as a reporter, I was working in New Orleans. I was a born-and-raised Texas boy with a thick Texas twang, so I do not begrudge anyone his accent.

Then I took the deposition of a Cajun African-American man who had worked in shipyards cleaning out huge tanks, which I believe gave him his raspy voice – as if I needed any more dimension to add to the difficulties I was having with his speech pattern.

I got back to my office, deeply disappointed in my inability as a court reporter to understand and record this witness' testimony. Most of the other 30 reporters who worked at my agency immediately could tell how wiped out, frustrated, and dejected I was without my having to utter a word.

One colleague came up to me and said, "Was the witness Cajun?" I looked up at her, startled. How could she possibly know that?

The others in the immediate area were standing around grinning and nodding. They told me all out-of-the-area reporters had to go through this baptism of fire. Then these New Orleans veterans all pitched in and helped me slog through the testimony, and together we got the transcript out.

The one phrase that stumped the entire group the longest was something that sounded like BO-WAU-SUH, which will give you an idea of the thickness of this witness' accent. It finally occurred to me that the witness had stopped and picked up some BUD-WEIS-ER beer.

Beware of Deponent

By Susie Salenger Smith, BS, RPR, CCR

One of the reasons I love this profession is because, with the exception of a few times, I can honestly say that I have never been bored. There are many more stories to be told, but this was one of my favorites.

I was asked to cover a depo in a very small town in the middle of nowhere. Being the adventurous person that I am, I said yes. Little did I know what I was in for. I was told that I needed to go to the deponent's home (and I use that term loosely) because he was very ill with cancer and could not travel to a lawyer's office.

Since this was before the advent of GPS, I must have driven by it about three times before I realized that that was indeed where I needed to be. I pulled up to the shack, a/k/a home, on a dirt road and was greeted by a passel of fairly large dogs surrounding my car and barking their rather substantial heads off. And, oh, by the way, there was also a horse that was actually lying in the front yard. I don't believe I have ever seen a horse in such a relaxed state. I hoped that he wasn't sick.

I waited in the car, of course, a little fearful of what the dogs might do. I tried to call the agency on my cell phone, but naturally there was no service out there. I'm not sure if my inability to contact my office was the result of the remote area I was in or the very heavy brick-type cell phone that I was using at that time.

Finally, the front door of the shack swung open. There he stood, a very skinny, very tan, not very ill-looking, middle-aged man. What was the most striking thing, however, was the fact that he was wearing nothing more than a Speedo, and sporting a large chest tattoo.

He walked over to the car, and in spite of how stunned I was, I allowed him to open my door. I surprised myself even more, as I allowed him to carry my machine for me as he escorted me inside the house. Luckily, the dogs stopped barking and allowed us to pass, and the horse was polite enough to stand as I walked by.

If I was not already shocked enough, the inside of the home did quite a number on my system. To call it a mess would be an understatement. There was actually no sheetrock up on the walls, but there was exposed insulation. At least he had the insulation going for him. I'm not really sure it would have mattered, though, since there was no air conditioning; not to mention that this was in South Florida in the middle of the summer.

He brought me to the kitchen and showed me where I would be seated for the depo. It was to be on a stool near the only phone in the house. At least he had the decency to cover the stool with a towel for me, but the phone was one that hung on the wall.

The fact that it was a speaker phone would have had no significance for me except for the fact that my agency conveniently neglected to inform me prior to my accepting the assignment that the attorneys, *all of them*, were appearing by phone.

Yay for me! I get to be alone in a house that should have been condemned, in the middle of nowhere, with a complete stranger wearing a Speedo. I was just praying that the deponent was not a serial killer interested in cutting up women and burying them in his back yard. I imagined the crime being solved when the police discovered all of my steno equipment stored in his garage.

Enough. I focused on the professional task at hand. I set up my machine, sat on my stool, waited for the attorneys to call, and took the depo. It was not that long, thank goodness, but it was long enough to have me sweating like a pig, the one animal that seemed to be missing in the garbage-strewn front yard.

When the deposition was over, I packed up at breakneck speed, got in my car with the assistance of my Speedo-clad friend, and drove straight home.

Upon arriving at my beautiful house with indoor walls and air conditioning, I did not even sit down. I immediately took my dress off and actually threw it away. I felt so sweaty and gross. All I wanted to do was to jump into the shower and wash any hint of the day away.

It is a depo that will forever be etched in my mind. Now that I have much more experience under my belt, I realize that I am allowed to say no, I'm not doing this, it is not an appropriate venue for a depo and I am not comfortable. I am amazed at the situations we are put in and we just say, okay, here I am at your service.

Susie Salenger Smith, BS, RPR, CCR, is currently working as an independent contractor reporter in Augusta, Georgia and the surrounding areas. She has a Bachelor of Science degree from Florida State University and followed in her mother Ellen's footsteps by becoming a court reporter. She graduated from Sheridan Vocational in Hollywood, Florida in 1989 as a court reporter, and has been reporting ever since.

She has worked in South Florida, Central Florida, Georgia, South Carolina, and had the privilege of reporting in Puerto Rico and the Cayman Islands. She is newly and very happily married to Doug Smith, and is the proud stepmom of 12-year-old Samuel. She enjoys cooking, singing, and taking care of her new family, which also includes her four-legged babies, Purdy, Zero, and Junior.

Reindeer Meatballs, Anyone?

By Carmelita Lee

I was privileged to follow one case for five months, and *follow* is the operative word. Let's just say the opposing parties, represented by multinational mega firms, were mega in their own right, manufacturers of telephones. "Somebody" copied "somebody else's" proprietary information, and now it was a huge patent infringement case. The adventures and misadventures of this case will probably never leave me.

I got a frantic call on a rare sunny day in Dublin, Ireland. I was lazing in my back yard lawn chair, wishing the Irish courts weren't closed for two months, wondering how I would meet the rent without borrowing from savings. The caller, one of my favourite agencies to work for, had moments before gotten a contract. "Can you go to Tampere, Finland? Tonight? For the next week? And could you take two depos in Copenhagen first? We've already started booking your flights."

Aaagh! I was slathered in sun block and my hair was a mess — no point in getting a fresh dye job when I won't be working until October, if you get my drift. I didn't even know where my husband was, or when he would be back. He had left his cell phone on the dining table.

So echoed the mantra of the court reporter into the phone: "Yes, I'll take your job. "

I was running inside the house as we spoke. I keep a suitcase ready in my office. I started slamdunking my realtime cables, my international power converters, started rounding up my little realtime computers. I keep everything labeled and in its own bag. My good friend Brenda had advised me many years ago to label them 1 through whatever, so that I would be sure everything got inside the case. It has turned out to be very good advice.

Some of the cables, wires, plug-ins, I have to keep with my machine case in the event that my luggage gets lost. That makes for a very heavy carry-on, I have to say. The good-looking young men who offer to lift it up into the overhead compartment for me always make that telltale "Ooof, what do you have in here, lady?" remark. "It's an office in a small case," I say, smiling with my best little-old-lady face. Those guys are my heroes, believe me.

I started grabbing my clothes. No time to analyze what to wear, or how hot, cold or in-between it would be in Finland; no way to look on the internet and browse around about the weather or what to see when I'm on free time. It's summer, hey, so okay. I pick my Phoenix, Arizona winter suits, the perfect weight for Dublin's summers. I have a check-off card, also the suggestion of my friend, and as I finalize everything – the passport is No. 1, of course – I am able to close the suitcase, purse, machine case and computer backpack knowing everything is inside.

The phone rang several times as the coordinator was giving me information on my ticket. All I had was my flight number and my reservation number. My husband had come in with his bag of groceries, and as I showered and washed my hair, he loaded the car. I ate my dinner as we drove to the airport.

Within two hours and ten minutes of the first call, I was boarding a flight to Copenhagen. It was 4:30. I was to take two depositions that night at an airport hotel, one the next day, and then board a flight to Finland. I didn't have a case caption, or any advance research about the suit.

When I landed in Copenhagen, a smaller airport, I could see the airport Hilton, and walked, dragging all the equipment. I settled into my room and then found the depo suite. We had about a half hour to spare. I met, for the first time, Joe, the somewhat eccentric videographer who was going to be my partner in crime for the next five months. He was finishing his setup procedures as I started testing the realtime, as surprised to be in Copenhagen as I.

I knew I was in trouble just after swearing in the witness. By then I realized this was about source code for camera phones. He had an inordinately long, Scandinavian name, and spoke English with a delightful accent, especially when asked what his profession was: "I am a computer scientist." Uh-oh.

Well, I didn't pass out, just muddled through. At every lull in the conversation I would throw the exotic spellings, names, and codes into my job dictionary. "The names of some of the circuitries inside your cellphone are *Vilma3_71.ah/r3Z>Fred.*" No joke. These engineering geniuses loved the Flintstones. (They just knew Mrs. Flintstone as Vilma rather than Wilma.)

When I realized that they might use a certain source code, or a certain sequence in the source code repeatedly, I made a brief on the fly, and these briefs served me for the whole five months. Those guys thought *I* was a genius!

The parties required realtime, a rough at the end of the depos, and daily copy. I used my excellent scopist in California to produce the transcripts, and I prayed she was getting a good sound feed. We used Dropbox for almost virtual realtime to her doorstep.

Without time to look at anything, we left the depo room on the second day and just made it onto our flight to Helsinki with minutes to spare. This would turn out to be the norm for the rest of our time on this job. I can't describe for you how many times I was running at full speed from one end of an airport to the other, only to be the last person on board, and once, to miss the flight entirely, arriving the very split second they closed the doors.

We were headed for Tampere, which is about 200 miles north of Helsinki. We had no instructions how to get there for the depositions which started at 8 a.m. the next day. We landed in Helsinki at 11 p.m.

There was a train, but its last north run of the night was already gone. There was a bus, but getting to the bus station was going to be a problem. The videographer and I ended up taking *a taxi for 200 miles.*

This trip saw a catastrophic failure of my main computer. I spent a sleepless night with Stenograph on the phone, jerry-rigging the computer to work again. A friend in Dublin was able to replace it by the time I was home. Video Joe told anti-Semitic jokes to a table full of Jewish lawyers (repeatedly). They would look at him and me with a blank stare, and I wanted so badly to say, "Listen, I just met him..."

And I had to eat...a reindeer meatball. It was gag awful. It actually ended up in tiny pieces in my napkin, in my purse, so that I wouldn't offend my gracious hosts. The hosts generally provided us five-star meals, but every meal in Scandinavia included reindeer. I came up with several creative ways to hide the entrée while I was up in that neck of the woods.

The case took me to Tampere five times, each time for a week; to Helsinki for depos; to the North Pole in a blinding snowstorm; to Oslo, Norway; to Stockholm, Sweden; to Copenhagen, Amsterdam and Brussels; to Frankfurt five times; to Munich twice (where I missed that flight to Stockholm); then to warmer climes, twice to Milan and once to Bologna, Italy; then a week in Portugal.

Other exciting mini-adventures I experienced in the course of reporting this case:

- I had to travel beside a wretching drunk, but thankfully was moved to another seat.
- I was almost arrested in Oulo, Finland (i.e., the North Pole) for being *underdressed*. Yes, granny was walking about in jeans and a sweatshirt, but no gloves, hat, boots or coat. "You'll have frostbite in 20 minutes," said the policeman, "and I order you inside."
- I rode a bus so crowded that I had to sit on the floor in the middle aisle for over a hundred miles.
- Oh, and Phoenix winter suits don't work in Finland. We got caught in the first snowstorm of the season – in late August – and I couldn't

convince Joe to take my photo with six inches of snow on my head, my backpack, and my machine case.

- I had to walk a mile to the train station with all my equipment because Joe was convinced it was "only 30 meters away," and we couldn't afford a taxi.

- We were caught in a fire. In the middle of a deposition, the command came over the public address system, "This is not a drill. Everyone must leave the building." The attorneys were panicked because I refused to leave the building without first packing up and taking my equipment.

Every time my phone rings and a reporting agency is on the other end, I remember the most interesting experiences of my life, and I prepare to say YES to the caller. Each trip out is an exciting and unique adventure.

Carmelita Lee has been a court reporter since 1983, and has been a published writer since 2001. She is a ghost writer for one of the preeminent barristers in Ireland, as well as his biographer and speech writer. She has a column in the Jerusalem Post entitled **Israel Lite**.

Growing up in a military family, Carm lived in Japan, Hawaii, France and all over the US. She married Raymond in 1963 and moved to Phoenix, then Utah, and ultimately California, where she reported in the US District Court for the Central District of California for 12 years.

The family moved from there to Tel Aviv in the mid-90s, and then to Ireland in 1999, where Carmelita works as a reporter in the Four Courts.

She is currently writing **Dear Daddy**, the biography of an Irish family, and in 2006 published **Ramblings Off The Record**, an irreverent look at life in court.

Vignette 6: Nap Time

By Maxyne Bursky, BA, RPR, CRR, CCR

This is yet another anecdote told to me by a reporter wishing to remain *highly* anonymous, but I felt it was too good to pass up.

The chuckle surrounding working for this particular senior judge was that any reporter in that courtroom had better have his readback skills sharply honed, because there would be an embarrassment of riches in that department. Judge Jones was 91 years young, a brilliant jurist for all of his career, and a workaholic. He was on the bench daily by 9:00 a.m. and retired for the day after 6:00 p.m., ready to hear motions both before and after trials that would exhaust a much younger person.

The theory was that Judge Jones got his rest *during* the hearings and trials over which he presided. Invariably, once the trial testimony commenced, this man, who at five-foot-two could barely be seen over the bench, fell asleep. If there were an objection made to a question in open court, the law clerk would, without expression, bang his fist quietly against the side of the bench, out of eyesight of attorneys or jurors, and Judge Jones would wake up.

Seamlessly, Judge Jones would turn to the reporter and ask her to read back the question. After readback, a ruling was made, and the testimony resumed. And so did the judge's nap.

Judge Jones never required lawyers coming in on motion calendar to recap the facts of their cases, as he seemed to always be on top of the issues. We figure the siestas he got during the day helped.

What Doesn't Kill You...

By Dianne Coughlin, RPR, RMR, CRR, RDR, CSR

When I first started my career in 1993, I made the decision that I would never say no to any assignment. Baptism by fire would be my mantra. Looking back, this was absolutely the best approach I could have taken, but I also must have been nuts.

The first depo I took was a breeze. It had to do with a refund from a beauty school. The second depo I took was of an oral and maxillofacial surgeon who was a native New Yorker talking at least 300 words per minute, with the questioning attorney appearing via telephone.

Six months into my new career, I was assigned my first realtime job. The depo was being videotaped, and the attorneys insisted that I sit behind and to the side of the expert witness so as not to block the videotaping. I would never allow that to happen now, but inexperience and a lack of confidence allowed it to happen that day.

This particular case involved a patent infringement on the microprocessing chip inside a hearing aid. Before the proceeding began, the attorney unfurled a technical schematic as long as the conference table. As I struggled to keep my nerves intact and attempted to decipher the technical lingo being thrown about, all I could think about was (1) not fainting, (2) wishing I were camping, and, (3) knowing they can't kill me.

Anyway, we proceeded with the depo, and although every untranslate on my screen put my stomach in knots, the attorney receiving the feed turned to me at the end of the day and said, "Thanks. That was just great," which taught me the invaluable lesson that attorneys are not looking at what they don't get, they are looking at what they do get. Doing something so challenging at the beginning of my career taught me early on that I can do anything as long as I give it 100 percent.

Dianne Coughlin, CRR, RDR, CSR grew up in St. Cloud, Minnesota, the sixth of twelve children. Upon becoming a licensed court reporter in 1993, Dianne began working and traveling extensively as a freelance reporter based out of the San Francisco Bay area, and currently works as an official reporter with the Sacramento Superior Court.

She is presently serving her third term as president of the Sacramento Official Court Reporters.

Vignette 7: The Bare Facts

By Maxyne G. Bursky, BA, RPR, CRR, CCR

A videographer I know and a reporter with whom he was assigned to work were tagged to go to a residential development – a compound, actually – for a deposition. They were tasked with meeting the questioning attorney and defending attorney in a conference room located in the compound's clubhouse. It was a nudist colony.

Upon entering the conference room, the reporter and video guy saw that the plaintiff had already seated himself expectantly at the far end of the conference table – naked.

"Is this where you want me?" Not looking up, the cameraman mumbled that that was fine. The reporter, stunned, began to set up at the *near* end of the table, eyes fixed on the floor.

When counsel came in, both tried unsuccessfully to persuade the witness to be videoed while clothed. It would be better for the jury, his lawyer pointed out.

On principle, however, the plaintiff refused. The miserable videographer approached the star of the show and merely draped the microphone around the guy's neck. There was just no lapel to be had.

The participants mentally adjusted to the situation at hand, and the videographer went on the record and made his customary preliminary announcement. After counsel identified themselves on the record, the reporter asked the witness to raise his right hand to take the oath.

Concerned about proper procedure, the plaintiff asked the hapless reporter, "Do I need to stand?"

As if in a finely rehearsed Greek chorus, the other four present shouted in unison, "**NOOOO!**"

Captioning...in Russian?

By Sheri Smargon, RMR, CRR, CBC, M.A.

I will never forget my first day "on the air" as a realtime captioner. I had been out of court reporting school for eight months and became part of a pilot project in Hillsborough County, Florida, where I live, that was given the mandate of providing captioning for the Board of County Commissioners. They are the governing body that legislates everything related to county services, from pothole repair to what businesses will receive a liquor license.

The request was made that the meeting be open-captioned. What this means is if you just turned on your TV to Government Access Television, the captions would automatically appear, no extra button-pressing necessary. If you didn't want to see captions, well, you're kind of out of luck.

I was part of a three-man team that had to prep, design and implement the captioning program. The theory was that if you could write on "that machine," you could caption. Unfortunately, we were the first county in the nation to attempt such a program, so we didn't even have a footprint to follow. We prepped and prepped, brought in a nationally respected court reporting legend to assess our skill levels, abilities and dictionaries. And we were given an emphatic, "They're not ready." Despite that assessment, we went live a few weeks later, November 6, 1992.

It was a day that will live in infamy (for me, anyway). My team was so new. It consisted of me, a newbie captioner and court reporter; a friend of mine from school, also a beginning captioner and court reporter; and a veteran court reporter, but one who had never captioned or realtimed anything before. We would take ten-minute turns, quickly swapping places with the captioner in "the hot seat." This was all done in front of a live audience, with the Commission actively conducting business.

When it came my turn to spring into action, I was shaking so badly, I just couldn't control my nerves...or my captions. The Commissioners could look up and see the captions scrolling by and would chuckle and point – in bemused admiration, I prayed. There were journalists and photographers and media present, not to mention Hard-of-Hearing and Deaf Community advocates. None of us wanted to let anyone down or embarrass ourselves or them.

At one point, however, while I was writing, the Chairman of the Commission interrupted a speaker to advise him, "You may want to speak slower. It's coming up in Russian up there." *Laughter. Lots of it.*

Of course, he was going 350 words per minute – at least in my mind. In reality, who knows? An overwhelming sense of vertigo compounded by an imminent panic attack seemed to make time warp. But I made it through my session, passed the captioning baton to another of my colleagues, and then watched her get flushed and panicked, sweat profusely beading up on her forehead.

After that meeting was over, I had our production department make a copy of that particular meeting for me so I could watch it again later. And, boy, those captions were awful! Even the Russians would have been confounded by what showed up on that screen.

It's amazing how far I've come. My teammates have moved onto bigger and better things, I'm sure, but I know we will forever cherish the memory of captioning in "Russian" for the American public!

Sheri Smargon, MA, RPR, RMR, CRR, CBC, has been a broadcast captioner for most of her 19-year career. She has captioned both national and international news, working in the United States as well as Australia.

She is a former chief examiner for the National Court Reporters Association, and is also a former member of NCRA's Realtime Certification Committee.

Ask Patty: Reporting Recommendations

By Patty Lee Hubble, RPR, RMR, CRR, RDR, CSR

When I started at Alameda County Superior Court in 1977 with a whole six months of deposition reporting (car accident and a couple Workers' Comp. cases) under my belt, I felt skilled, professional, and ready to tackle any assignment.

My first job was reporting for a judge during his last two weeks on the bench before starting a new career as the mayor. They wouldn't give him any difficult cases, he assured me, he was just biding his time. It turned out to be a bench trial. "Great," he told me, "We won't have to worry about a jury."

It turned out there were other things for me to worry about. It was a homicide case where the infant was the victim. The first witness was the coroner.

The lights were dimmed to show the autopsy slides. No one had bothered to cull out any photos of the baby's skull as there was no jury. I turned green and slid off my seat. It took a while for me to regain my composure, and everyone was very understanding.

Recommendation 1: Stay in your seat.

1994: Having a good relationship with my scopist, it is easy to vent by writing parenthetical notes to him while in a particularly tedious or annoying deposition. Comments such as, "Dude thinks he's too cool for his shirt," or, "If he reads that passage one more time, I'm going to throw up," would serve to amuse him in the course of producing the transcript. I think that venting is a very good thing, a nice stress reliever. A practice like this does have its down side, however.

Recommendation 2: Make sure your office does not send out rough drafts (*un*reviewed by your scopist) without your knowledge. That could be a real sticky wicket.

1996: In Austria, I was privileged to be captioning an international seminar on disabilities. As was the custom, the speaker at the podium finished his formal presentation and asked the audience if there were any questions.

Several in the audience raised their hands to be recognized. The speaker, however, was blind. Dejected by the lack of apparent response, the speaker turned to leave the stage. I quickly darted from my station and intercepted his departure to get him to return to the podium. Then I ran back and captioned a lively question-and-answer session with this lecturer.

Recommendation 3: There are times you have to ignore Recommendation 1.

2011: I'm still in court and once again find myself reporting a homicide. I think back on all those embarrassing moments and wonder how I survived them, my professionalism intact.

Recommendation 4: Relax and keep your sense of humor, as well as your sense of humanity. There's always going to be another odd situation around the corner.

Patty Lee Hubble, RPR, RMR, CRR, RDR, CSR, has been a court reporter since 1977. She worked in Alameda County, California Superior Court until 2003, and took part in a job share program from 1984 to 2003 that allowed her the opportunity to report depositions as well as caption. She was an official at the Superior Court for San Francisco just before retiring this year.

Patty presented seminars from 1997 to 2002 regarding realtime tips and tricks in various parts of the country. She has been on the National Court Reporters Association's Realtime Certification Committee, the Membership Telemarketing Committee, and the Council of CAPR Test Advisory Committee.

Patty is a certified clinical hypnotherapist, neurolinguistic programming professional, emotional freedom technique practitioner, and president of California Virtual Gastric Band.

Vignette 8: You Want Me Where?? When???

By Donald J. White, RPR, RMR, CSR

Part of the duty of a Nassau County, New York Grand Jury reporter back in 1962 was to provide reporting services to the DA's office for homicide statements, and to be on call for same, as well as all other DA investigations requiring a record.

On February 19, 1962 at 2:30 a.m., I was called to the Long Beach Police Department where I was met by the Assistant DA in charge of the homicide bureau. With him were the chief of detectives, the chief of homicide, and the police commissioner, all of Long Beach.

A homicide had taken place at the Long Island Railroad depot about an hour before, and the alleged shooter was Earl Miller, a known criminal in the area.

All four of these officials had been in attendance at a law enforcement dinner earlier that evening, and even though they had not been specifically called to duty to cover this investigation, since they were already together, and the police had a good tip where Miller was hiding, they opted to join forces to apprehend him.

I was crammed into a large unmarked vehicle with the other fellows, and we sped off down the boardwalk toward the location where the suspect was supposed to be holed up. My adrenal gland was pumping furiously, and even more so when one of the chiefs exclaimed, "Wait a minute. I don't have a gun!"

We all soon realized that no one among us had a weapon, so the speeding car slowed while a better course of action was planned. As it turned out, I was the only one with the tools of my trade that night, ready to record the Q & A. But cooler heads prevailed and we returned to the station.

After little sleep that night, I had a full day of Grand Jury proceedings. Then Miller was apprehended the following evening, and I returned to Long Beach where he was fully interrogated and confessed – all on the record.

Until the use of video statements, for over twenty years, Grand Jury or confidential reporters in Nassau County testified in open court regarding the statements they reported, including reading from stenographic notes against transcripts. None of those statements was ever overturned by an appellate court. That reporter success rate has never been matched by video statements.

Sweat Equity: Reporting in Trinidad and Tobago

By Beulah Dalrymple

My odyssey in the reporting field has been an interesting one. To be a verbatim reporter in Trinidad and Tobago in the year 1991 meant shorthand (written or palantype machine) at a speed of 140 words per minute to act. To be considered for appointment, however, the required speed was reduced from 180 words per minute to 160 words per minute. I started with the acting requirement of 140 words per minute.

Within a week, I was ready to pack my bags and run out of the Industrial Court where I was acting. The writing time of each reporter was and still is at the Industrial Court, fifteen minutes per session. With a speed of 140 words per minute, and the speech rate of some attorneys at 200 words per minute, the frustration quickly mounted. The recorded back-up system was my saviour for the most part, failing which I would go into anxiety attacks, cold sweats, and dizzy spells.

My baptism of fire came when one of the judges, whose normal pitch was a whisper, requested that I read back a portion of the notes. I tried! I really did!! I got maybe the first three words, then I was silent. I didn't cry, but I was choking.

The judge, realising I was unable to read back, admonished me to stop the Court to ensure I get the record. I could feel myself melting in my chair. It was the longest fifteen minutes of my life.

I stumbled out of Court when I was relieved by another reporter, went back to my work station, packed my things and was out of Industrial Court for what I thought would have been forever. I knew that I was the talk of the Court.

But I was encouraged to stay. I was told these things happen. My regret was that it happened to me! I made it my duty to increase my writing speed. I did. I increased it to 160 words per minute. This is still shorthand, not machine writing.

During the year 1994, I decided to switch writing instruments. I became interested in the stenograph machine which was introduced into Trinidad and Tobago somewhere around 1987. I was unable to attend the institution at which the training for the machine was conducted, so I purchased a manual machine from the US, got a copy of the StenEd theory, and thus my journey into machine shorthand began.

Within a year of completing the theory and starting to build speed, I boldly took my machine and my recorder into Court, with not even a first level certifying speed of 100 words per minute – I had no speed. I also took my shorthand notebook, just in case the going got tough, which at times it did, and then I would quickly switch to my notebook and write shorthand. My supervisor, seeing my swift progress, advised me not to take my notebook in, but stick to the machine.

I took my machine everywhere I went. It was left open at all times. When I woke in the night to go to the bathroom I would take a few minutes and practise in the dark! When I visited the United States on vacation, I took my machine and practised. I took it to Venezuela as well when I was vacationing there.

I started taking private reporting jobs. One day, a senior reporter told me about the shorthand association in the States. I joined the NCRA, and from there onwards, I became interested in realtime writing and advancing technologically in the reporting field. I wanted to take the Industrial Court into realtime.

My NCRA Journal gave me the ability to do just that. I attended realtime workshops and continued to improve my skills by realtiming to myself in Court and on private jobs. On one of my big jobs, covering a Commission of Enquiry that was high-profile and televised, I was asked to read back a portion of notes. By that time, my self-confidence was pretty okay, but this is television you're talking about here; I was not about to chance an embarrassment. I quickly slipped the headset over my head, pointed to the position to be read back, and listened to my audio-sync while I read confidently. Oh, yes, I had it all right, but you never can tell what an onset of "nervousness" can do to a perfectly transcribed piece.

Reporting continues to excite and motivate me. My last tested speed was 200 words per minute. Having started as a self-taught stenograph machine reporter and advancing to the person at the Industrial Court who implemented a full realtime courtroom, I would say, realtime writing and court reporting in Trinidad and Tobago is my niche.

Beulah Dalrymple has been reporting in Trinidad and Tobago since 1991, first as a pen writer and then trained in 1994 to be a machine writer. She works in the Industrial Court as a realtime reporter, and has taken depositions and other assignments in the field of verbatim reporting.

She has been a member of the National Court Reporters Association since 2001.

E.T., Stay Home

By Maxyne G. Bursky, BA, RPR, CRR, CCR

In my present position, I have the opportunity of driving all over creation to report depositions. My assignments are not only in the metropolitan area, but also range into the suburbs and rural regions outside of Atlanta. I love the rich variety of scenery I travel through, as well as the contrasts in culture and lifestyle that I encounter.

One witness examination landed me in a tiny, rural Georgia town in the spring. Chrysanthemums, crepe myrtles, and peach blossoms crowded the front yards of the houses I passed. As I walked to the tiny town hall across the square from where I had parked, a few chickens were making their way along the sidewalk. This was a far cry from the 30-story tower in Atlanta I had worked in the day before. I am drawn to the potential adventures this job promises, and diversity in venue is part of that.

Apparently, the office out of which my agency's client practiced either could not accommodate all four of us, or his meeting room was already taken up by some other matter. At any rate, the oversized conference room in town hall, with its impressive 25-foot wooden table, was home to our little proceeding that day.

This case involved a grandmother suing to gain custody of her nine-year-old granddaughter. Grandma was alleging that her daughter, a single mom and resident of big, bad Atlanta, was an unfit parent. Mom pushed back on that notion, and so a lawsuit was born.

The interrogation began with the usual questions: name, address, education, etc. Granny was a tiny, blue-haired member of the local garden club and an elder in her church. She was convinced that life in a small town is far superior to that in a big city, especially when it comes to raising a child.

She claimed that things were so safe in her corner of the world that no one ever locked their doors. "In fact," she continued, quite animated, "every night I back my car on up my driveway and two aliens hop in the back seat and throw a force field around my house. Nobody can get in or out until dawn."

You could have heard a pin drop. I could not believe what I had just heard. Needless to say, the attorney representing this lively senior became somewhat pale and ashen. "Off the record," he announced.

"Not just yet. I have a few more things to ask," my client stated, his voice not revealing one iota of surprise at the information the witness had just provided. And we all know, based on previous chapters, that if the attorneys voice disagreement with going off the record, the reporter stays on the record. This is how the rest of the transcript looked:

Q.   What do you mean by "aliens"? Are they people from another country?

A.   Of course not. They're from outer space.

Q.   How do you know they're from outer space?

A.   By their paper hats, their beak noses, and their gold dresses, of course.

MR. CLIENT: Okay, now we can go off the record.

MR. OTHER ATTORNEY: Thank you very, very, very much.

Needless to say, as Granny and her attorney made a hasty exit from the conference room, the latter mumbled something about withdrawing the lawsuit with prejudice (who would have guessed that one?).

With the deposition adjourned and the other party gone, I smiled at the questioner, and told him I assumed that he would not want this transcribed.

"Oh, no. You *must* get this to me. I want to frame it and hang it in my office!" I guess an alien sighting was something of a novelty to him. We court reporters hear about everything else, so why not throw a story of a rural Klingon into the mix.

Vignette 9: Laid-Back Reporting Attire

By Jacqueline M. Timmons, RPR, RMR, RDR, CSR, FAPR

I was traveling to Taiwan for a deposition, so I wore a long t-shirt and jean-type leggings to be comfortable for my approximately 15-hour flight and to make lugging all my equipment between connections that much easier. I had two laptops and my court reporting machine, and all the accessories for realtime, so there was no room to pack extra clothing in my carry-on.

Unfortunately, due to a delay in my departure out of Chicago, I missed the connecting flight in Hong Kong. I was put on a different airline, but my luggage was not. I arrived in Taiwan around midnight with just my equipment, a small bag, and my smile.

After filling out a lost luggage report, I left the airport, arriving at my hotel around 2:00 a.m. I had to be downstairs in the conference room at 7:00 a.m. to set up, so there was no time to shop for clothes. Fortunately, I had been on the same case two weeks earlier, so when I arrived this time at the deposition in my Tweety Bird shirt and denim leggings, the attorneys knew that this was not my usual attire.

Thank goodness my luggage arrived later that afternoon. I now travel in comfortable clothing, but something that would be presentable in the event my luggage is delayed or lost.

There Are No Words

By Kenneth McClure, BA, RPR, RMR

September 11, 2001, was not the first time the World Trade Center was the object of a terrorist attack. On February 26, 1993, a car bomb was detonated in a subbasement parking garage in the North Tower. Its horrific intent was also to bring both towers down. This first time, although the devil was cheated, six people were killed and 1,042 injured.

On the afternoon of the bombing, I was in a small courtroom on the first floor of the old Manhattan Federal Courthouse, reporting a routine civil trial, which recessed when the crescendo of sirens flooding downtown Manhattan made it impossible to hear the testimony. By September of 1993, the first of three related "bomber trials" (USA v. Omar Abdel-Rahman, and three others) was beginning before Judge Kevin

Thomas Duffy, in a grand courtroom before a packed house.

Two-reporter teams covered daily copy trials in our courthouse, one reporter relieving the other at 45-minute intervals. There were two chairs by the reporter's table, and the trick was to enter unobtrusively, set up your stenographic machine, wait for an appropriate moment, signal your associate, and start to write. We prided ourselves on doing this seamlessly. And seamlessly, I thought, it had been done.

I entered midstream into a blistering cross-examination of a government witness, and was pounding my keyboard to capture every phoneme. But I hadn't secured the folding legs which anchor my stenographic machine; one of them was only partly extended and thus vulnerable to collapse. And in the middle of counsel's question, before an otherwise hushed courtroom, it did collapse. Very loudly. And stopped the show.

Judge Duffy paused the proceedings while, insofar as possible, I reassembled my composure and the tools of my trade. Counsel wondered if the last question might be read back. The Judge considered the ruination of my steno notes, now strewn in a heap of irredeemable chaos, and said: "Nah, I don't think so."

* * *

The five-month trial would include other humiliating moments in which the court reporter was not the principal actor. On December 8, 1993, a gas station attendant who was to implicate several defendants, when called upon to point them out, eschewed the defendants' table where the alleged conspirators sat so conspicuously and turned his scrutiny resolutely upon the jury box, identifying two jurors as the culprits.

Nevertheless, on March 4, 1994, having listened to the testimony of 207 prosecution and four defense witnesses, after deliberating for five days, the jury found the defendants guilty on all counts, including conspiracy, explosive offenses, and assault.

Born in 1949, Ken McClure, BA, RPR, RMR, received his Bachelor of Arts degree from New York University in 1972. Since that time, he has worked as both an official and freelance court reporter in New York, freelancing as well in Vermont and South Carolina.

Ken and his wife Kathi owned and operated a bookstore in Montpelier, Vermont. In addition to Ken's court reporting endeavors, the McClures currently run McClure's Bookstore in Clemson, South Carolina.

All the World Was Watching

By Dianne Coughlin, RPR, RMR, CRR, RDR, CSR

On September 11, 2001, I arrived at a hotel in Taipei for a week of depositions. I turned on CNN just at the moment that the second attack on the World Trade Center was occurring.

My first thought was that it was the Petronas Twin Towers in Kuala Lumpur, Malaysia, where I had spent time. I then realized in even more stunned horror that it was New York.

I immediately called the attorney I was with. She paused a moment after I delivered the news, then said, "Dianne, you must be really tired after that long flight. Why don't you get some rest and call me later." Only seconds passed and she called me back, frantic, and we tried to come to grips with this shocking tragedy.

A decision was made that the parties would meet in the morning to decide how to proceed. When we all arrived in the conference room the next day, the Taiwanese host attorney was very gracious, and offered that if we wanted to postpone the depositions, they would be agreeable to doing so. However, since all air travel was indefinitely suspended, the consensus was to go forward as scheduled.

I must admit, it was very difficult staying focused, keeping the concentration level high, in the midst of this global crisis. Throughout the week, there was a palpable sense of uncertainty among the Americans staying in the hotel. It was unnerving. Everyone kept their heads down and avoided speaking with or acknowledging each other.

When the depositions finally concluded, we waited three more days before there was any flight out of Taiwan. United Airlines was the first airline to restore service to the US, and we boarded a 747 bound for home with fewer than 30 passengers aboard.

Three weeks later, I received a call asking if I would go to Stockholm for a series of depos. I said yes immediately, packed my bags, and off I went. Despite the tense atmosphere surrounding international air travel at that time, I resolved never to let the threat of terrorism stop me.

Breaking the Cycle of Violence

By Roy Isbell, RPR, RMR, RDR, CRR

I turned back to the two men seated outside the judge's office. "Excuse me, aren't you Morris Dees?" They were seated on a small loveseat. Dees looked up from his reading. I introduced myself, adding, "I'm the court reporter that did all those Klan depositions for you a couple of years ago." Both men smiled.

I had been at the bottom of the heap at the freelance firm that assigned me to those depositions back in November 1984. When I had arrived at the hotel as instructed, no one there knew the contact name I'd been given or anything about a deposition. I was about to rush back to our office to check the scheduling book for a contact number when a man stopped me. "Are you here for the deposition?" He led me through the courtyard and down an iron-laced veranda.

The Malaga Inn was made up of a couple of renovated townhouses from antebellum days on a quiet, oak-lined street. Room 007 was big and dark, sparsely decorated with well-worn antiques, including a gilt pier mirror and crystal chandelier. It was just after 8 a.m. Several men lounged around the room as I set up. When I requested their names for the record, they hesitated, then said it wasn't important to note their presence, that they were not participating. *Okay.* Attorney Morris Dees was tall and thin and moved silently about the room. His assistant, Bill Stanton, chatted affably with the other men as we waited. No one appeared for the defense.

When the first deponent finally arrived and testimony began, the men who "weren't participating" stood around leaning against the door frames, quietly observing. The mundane questioning gradually turned to a night in March 1981, and Dees zeroed in on the death of a black teen which had been in the news a lot. Several grand juries had questioned residents from the run-down neighborhood in midtown where the body was found, so some of the deponents seemed familiar to me. Now Dees of the Southern Poverty Law Center in Montgomery was suing the United Klans of America in federal court and reliving the case in a hotel room in Mobile, Alabama.

Denise Hays, estranged wife of Henry, testified that her husband and several other men had played cards at her home the night of the murder. Around dawn, Henry claimed to have discovered a body hanging in a tree across the street. Denise suspected their involvement. Other witnesses added bits and pieces to the story.

About halfway through the day, Dees reached up and poked a finger between the buttons on the front of his shirt. The scratch made a peculiar, Velcro-like sound. He was wearing a bulletproof vest. No one had warned me there might be danger involved. Typical.

Dees deposed seven witnesses by 6:05 p.m. I had just gotten back to our office in the Commerce Building when the attorneys called again, asking me to run to the federal courthouse, a block away, for a depo they had not told me about. It was 6:15 p.m. when I got there. The witness was in the custody of the US Marshal, and two deputies were putting on rubber gloves, preparing to frisk us. Bill Stanton braced himself and stepped forward, pretending to be nonchalant. I was horrified.

We proceeded to a small conference room, where we were met by the attorney for the United Klans, John Edmond Mays. Then the marshals brought in Tiger Knowles. Knowles had been a short, plump 17-year-old when he was a new recruit of Unit 900. Belonging to the Klan gave him a sense of purpose. He admired the leaders and followed their wishes. Only a couple of years had passed, but he looked much older. He gave a vivid recitation of the abduction of Michael Donald from a city street at gunpoint, the drive across the bay, where the victim was murdered, and how the body was brought back downtown and hanged from a tree.

Afterward, Dees and Stanton talked with deputies while I took the elevator down to the front door and waited with Mays for someone to unlock it. I was thinking I'd have to guard my machine with my life until I got safely back to the office. When no one came to let us out, we pressed the red release button and went out onto the front steps. We parted ways in the growing darkness.

At mid-afternoon the following day, we took the deposition of Henry Hays' father, Bennie Hays, the second highest-ranking member of the United Klans, in his jail cell. The irascible old man had been arrested for insurance fraud, accused of burning his home to pay his son's attorney. He was one of the few witnesses who had counsel, and we all sat on two cots in the tiny cell. Hays ranted about his daughter-in-law, "the lying bitch," for giving statements incriminating his son.

Dees had handed me a couple of exhibits before we began, which I left lying on the bed when Hays swung his cane at Dees and the guards hustled us out. After I realized my mistake, I turned to Stanton and said: "The exhibits." He calmly enlisted a guard to retrieve them. I felt embarrassed, but relieved to get them back intact.

* * *

We completed Hays' examination and drove to the courthouse for the deposition of his wife, Opal. She presented a stack of Klan literature several feet tall. The UKA was a paramilitary organization, and its structure was detailed completely in the records.

I don't remember if the following incident took place the same night of Tiger Knowles' deposition or the next. I was leaving the federal building and crossing St. Joseph Street, my steno case in my left hand. Dusk was about to settle in. I passed a closed bank and headed toward the steady lights of my destination one block away. I left the sidewalk, crossing through the half-empty block diagonally, toward the center of the Commerce Building.

I had read somewhere that a gentleman walking down a sidewalk should cross the street to avoid meeting a woman walking alone. It would be politically incorrect to say a white man on a deserted street might feel a similar uneasiness at the approach of a group of black men, and normally I would feign indifference and continue walking. However, when the battered old car pulled up Royal Street and stopped between me and my destination, I stopped short of the sidewalk.

Hand in your pocket. I slipped my right hand inside and clutched my keys. *Look them square in the eye.* The car windows were down. *What are they saying? It doesn't make any sense.*

Directions to the post office? I couldn't think where it was, but I glanced to the right, then to the left. I knew it was in that direction to the left. Yes, over there. I could almost see the end of the street three blocks away. *"Stay on this street,"* I said steadily. *"It ends right down there. That's the back of the post office."*

"I can't hear what you said. Can you come here?"

I don't move. A narrow pole is slightly to the side, if I have to put something between us. I repeat firmly, *"You go that way until the street dead-ends at the back of the post office. Turn left and it takes you around to the front."*

They wait. I don't cross the sidewalk, though. I'm not so trusting anymore. I stare back at them, blood pounding in my ears. Then they drive on. I watch them go one block and then disregard my directions totally. They turn and speed away.

On Tuesday, February 10, 1987, the federal trial began before the Honorable Alex T. Howard, Jr., in the large ceremonial courtroom lined with portraits of past judges. Beulah Mae Donald, the victim's mother, sat stoically beside Dees at the head of the plaintiff's table.

Tiger Knowles recounted in graphic detail the night of the abduction, the drive across the bay to a swampy area in rural Baldwin County, where the frightened boy was taunted and beaten, pleaded for his life, fought back, escaped, was overpowered, beaten again and choked with a noose around his neck, dragged face-down in the dirt. His throat was cut three times and the body returned to Mobile and prepared for all the world to see. There the klansmen retired to Hays' home and played cards until dawn, as giddy as children waiting for Christmas morning.

The evidence closed on the second day at 3:30 p.m. Mr. Mays presented no defense. Judge Howard commented to the law clerks and me in chambers that Mobile had never experienced the kind of overt racial violence as had other Alabama towns. Founded in 1702, the port city had had a large Creole and free black population. It was not uncommon to see a black man and a white man seated on the same bench together in Bienville Square. The kind of atrocity committed against Michael Donald was by hate mongers on the fringes of society.

A news item during that time frame told of a white teenager being attacked by two black men in a schoolyard in west Mobile. The story got very little coverage. The 16-year-old had been running alone on the track field and had had his throat cut from ear to ear. Left for dead, he kept his chin clamped down and had not bled to death.

The third day of trial, Dees presented his closing argument. Tiger Knowles also addressed the jury, asking them to find him and the others guilty. Turning to Mrs. Donald, he begged her forgiveness. Jurors wept openly. At 7:10 p.m., the all-white jury returned a verdict in favor of Mrs. Donald and assessed punitive damages at $7 million. The Klan was financially destroyed. Proceeds from the sale of the Klan headquarters bought Mrs. Donald the first home she ever owned.

Much has been written of these events and of the strategy of applying the doctrine of agency to the Ku Klux Klan. The case has been called the last lynching in America. The trial was depicted in several movies and books. Morris Dees sent me an autographed copy of his own book and asked me to speak with a producer about appearing in the TV film. I videotaped the movie to watch someday as time permitted.

Mrs. Donald died in 1988, roughly a year and a half after the civil trial. Henry F. Hays was convicted of murder in state court and executed June 6, 1997.

There was one other thing – something so disturbing that I immediately put it out of my mind and refused to think about until years later. After the assault of the white boy, I caught a brief newscast on TV about the sentencing hearing for an assailant. The face was unforgettable.

The defendant gave law enforcement a complete statement and admitted that before the attack, they had driven their battered old car downtown, all around the post office, looking for a white man to kill in retaliation. But they only found one on Royal Street, who wouldn't come close enough to the car and might have had a weapon in his pocket.

Roy Isbell, RPR, RMR, RDR, CRR, received an Associate in Applied Science in court reporting from Gadsden State Junior College in 1981. A member of NCRA since 1981, he became a Registered Professional Reporter in 1983, Registered Merit Reporter in 1986, and received the Certified Realtime Reporter and Registered Diplomate Reporter designations in 1994. In 1986, he joined the US Federal Court for the Southern District of Alabama, serving Chief Judge Alex T. Howard, Jr., until the judge's retirement in 2001; and since 2002 has been assigned to Chief Judge Callie V. S. Granade.

In 1983, Roy was married to Debra S. Amos, RPR, RMR, RDR, CRR, owner of a freelance firm in Mobile, Alabama. They have two children.

Attorney Antics

By Kelly McKee, RPR, CRR, CCR

It was the beginning of my senior year of high school, and I had decided to attend court reporting school at the American Institute of Business in Des Moines, IA. Two weeks after graduation I left my small hometown of Bowling Green, MO, and trekked the 250 miles to begin my education for what I had no idea at the time would be a life-changing career.

Upon graduation in 1986 I had offers of employment stretching from Honolulu, Hawaii to Hartford, Connecticut to Savannah, GA; however, having no ties to anything, I settled on the Southeast. The freelance court reporting firm I went to work for was an internationally known firm specializing in large maritime disasters.

My boss, the firm's namesake, was from the court reporting generation of dictating paper notes for a transcriber to produce his work. He had a driver and would read his stenographic shorthand notes into a tape recorder while being driven to and from depositions all over South Georgia. He was a wildly vivid, entertaining gentleman who would treat us to fine dining and tales of his maritime travel after a long day of depositions. These tales and this lifestyle soon made me realize that I wanted to attain this status as well.

After several years of car accidents and Workers' Compensation cases (what I considered my on-the-job training) I landed my own case. This is where my life and outlook for my future began to change.

The case was a products liability lawsuit, and it involved companies from all over: Georgia, California, Texas, Pennsylvania; even a Belgian-based company was involved. The depositions in this case lasted over a year and included extensive travel.

I myself was garnering experience daily. I was learning that each lawyer has his or her own way of conducting a deposition, a sort of method to their madness. For example, one of the plaintiff's lawyers was an aged, hard-of-hearing solo practitioner who had partnered with one of Savannah's premier, most aggressive law groups. Mr. Smith used to like to go for the shock factor.

On a trip to Cleveland, at dinner he asked the maitre d' if they had dried possum on the menu. Shaking my head, I just played the quiet role and pretended I wasn't at the same table.

The next day during the deposition, I was in a room full of senior lawyers, associates and French witnesses. This group of highly educated litigators decided – without consulting me, of course – that they would just raise their hands when they had an objection. The plan was then for me to insert the objection into the transcript, all the while recording the continuing Q & A along with possibly verbalized objections.

The fact that the lead questioner was the aforementioned hard-of-hearing attorney just added to the idiocy of this idea, since no matter what was going on around him – objections, testimony, fire alarms – he just kept right on talking.

It finally occurred to me that I only had two hands, two ears and one brain, and the sort of simultaneous multi-tasking they were expecting from me was out of the question. When I tried to say something, Smith ignored me, or didn't even hear me.

Not that long after the deposition began, I had reached my limit of tolerance. I hammered my hand on the massive conference room table, and the entire room fell to a hush! All eyes were on me. Even Mr. Smith looked over. From their shocked expressions, one could assume that they had never heard a court reporter speak during a proceeding. I took a deep breath and addressed the hushed audience: "*Please* make your objections one at a time, and they *have* to be verbalized." I returned my gaze to my notes, waiting for the next question to be uttered, with a newfound sense of power over the record!

In another deposition in the case, being held on a Saturday, I met one of my now-lifelong friends. She was a first-year associate who went to work for one of the most well-respected attorneys in the group. When she made her first objection ever, good old Mr. Smith responded, "I'm sorry. Did you say something, *little lady*?"

One of the other plaintiff's counsel, Mr. Jones, whose mood you could tell by whether he had brushed his hair before the deposition, was a get-to-the-point kind of guy. He would blast into the deposition room and start firing questions to the witness before even sitting down. Never mind those little details of swearing in the witness and discussing stipulations; let's *git-'er-done*.

I remember for one such deposition, we had traveled to Atlanta to meet with the witness. Jones walked into the room, we quickly went on the record, and his first question was, "Who shot Roger Rabbit?" Serious as a heart attack, he waited patiently for the incredulous witness to respond. He followed up with four or five more questions and then walked out, declaring the deposition over as he left.

Kelly McKee, RPR, CRR, CCR, has been a court reporter since 1986. In 1992, she started McKee Court Reporting in Savannah, Georgia and ran the company until 2006.

Every year since 1996 she has provided instantaneous transcript of player interviews at the week-long Family Circle Cup tennis tournament in Hilton Head Island, South Carolina.

Kelly is also attending Armstrong Atlantic State University in Savannah, Georgia, pursuing a psychology and sports medicine degree. She is presently with Savannah Court Reporting.

Vignette 10: Returning from the Grave

By Gene Lee, CSR-TX

I'm in the middle of writing the testimony of a criminal defendant, and his attorney asks the man what happened to him back before he committed the current offense. The defendant states, "I killed myself."

Completely startled, his attorney looks up and says, "Excuse me?" The defendant reiterates his answer.

His lawyer, pursuing this bizarre line, asks how he had killed himself. The defendant explains he had committed suicide using a wire hanger around his neck.

"No further questions, your Honor." Naturally, the DA had a few things to ask.

"So if you killed yourself back then, how is it you're still alive now?" I thought to myself, I've been doing this too long. If I'm the State's Attorney, that's not a question I want to ask if I want to keep the defendant considered sane at the time of the current offense. But I'm just the lowly court reporter, I reminded myself.

The witness replied calmly, without the slightest hesitation: "Oh, I thought I told you. I killed myself back then, but then I needed to come back to commit this robbery here."

Either that defendant was a brilliant man or he really was insane. Nevertheless, the State's Attorney should have followed the classic advice, never ask a question you don't already know the answer to. The last I heard, the defendant still hadn't been tried for that robbery.

Lessons Learned the Hard Way

By Charlotte C. Roche, RPR, RMR, RDR, CRR, CSR

Once upon a time at a deposition, an attorney, we'll call her Ms. Smith, held in her hand an original document that would become Exhibit A; however, it needed to be copied and marked later so as not to alter or compromise the integrity of the original. It was clearly described, identified and referred to as Exhibit A. A few minutes later, Exhibit B was described the same way, to be marked after copying.

When we were off the record, I traipsed upstairs to Ms. Smith's office to get a copy. What was provided to me was not the same as what was described on the record. Ah, yes, the old switcheroo.

This was illegal, unethical, underhanded, and downright wrong. I checked my steno notes and found the exact dates of the documents, the "to," the "from," the page count and other features described. Then I insisted on getting the correct documents.

Ms. Smith learned some valuable lessons. Don't mess with the court reporter. We are officers of the court, and we're also no dummies.

Ms. Smith remained a client of our office for some time after that. When Judy, a colleague of mine, was assigned to report another deposition for this attorney, Smith called the police on the reporter! While off the record during a recess, and while Ms. Smith was out of the room, opposing counsel, Mr. Jones, asked Judy to take down some testimony.

Judy nervously suggested waiting until Smith returned to the conference room. But Jones insisted. He proceeded by asking the witness to make responses in what was hardly a question-and-answer session.

That's when Ms. Smith came back. She was furious. She called the cops! The police came and took a statement from everyone involved. Worse yet, the policeman decided to take Judy's steno machine and laptop into custody as a result of the incident.

Judy begged him to change his mind about confiscating her equipment. She explained to him this was her livelihood and that it also contained the transcript. Thankfully, she convinced him to let her pack up and leave, and she did so with lightning speed, lest the cop change his mind again!

Ms. Smith never used our agency after that, so none of us ever saw her again.

Word to the wise (and not so wise): If ever someone wants to put *any* sort of statement on the record, make sure all counsel are present in the room. No judge would permit ex parte statements in court. Reporters and attorneys alike are officers of the court, and as such, even in a company conference room, a deposition proceeding is to be conducted as if it were right smack dab in the middle of the courtroom.

Charlotte C. Roche, RPR, RMR, CRR, RDR, CSR, has been the owner of Bay Area Court Reporters in Hayward since 1985. Prior to that, Char was a staff reporter for a deposition firm in Oakland, California from 1979 until 1985. She became interested in court reporting when a family friend who was attending court reporting school brought that little machine to the house.

It was important for Charlotte to pursue a more specific education that would focus on learning the skills necessary to provide a long-term career. "The past 33 years in this occupation have truly been interesting and fulfilling in more ways than simply professionally and intellectually," she declares. "We meet people from all walks of life, feel rewarded when we are able to help others, and we really love that machine!"

Vignette 11: Look, Ma, No Files!

By Jacqueline M. Timmons, RPR, RDR, FAPR, CSR

At a deposition taken in Germany, due to some electrical issues, the motherboard on my writer was blown. I did not have a spare writer with me, because on a prior trip out of the country I packed a spare which had to be checked, and it was damaged, despite wrapping it in bubble wrap and putting it in one case inside of another.

Since I did have steno paper, I set my writer to write in manual mode and was able to report the deposition. Once I was back in the States, I restroked my notes on another writer so I could edit and send out my transcript. The most important lesson is to be flexible – and to breathe! You never know what you will encounter from assignment to assignment.

Vignette 11-1/2: Good News and Bad News

By Maxyne G. Bursky, BA, RPR, CRR, CCR

The good news is that the attorneys got their transcript on time in spite of the circumstances.

The good news is that Mary's 70-year-old mom wanted her month-long visit with her court reporter daughter and son-in-law to be a stress-free one. Her mother washed the dishes, vacuumed the house – in short, made herself useful while Mary was out working.

The neutral news is that Mary mentioned in passing that she needed to get a new battery for her computer, as it had been a while since she had replaced it, and she didn't want to get caught in the middle of a depo with a blank screen.

The bad news is that while Mary was out shopping, her mom figured out how to open the battery section of the computer. To be super-helpful, Mom also figured out how to cram a bunch of Eveready batteries into the battery compartment and squeeze it closed. What a nice surprise it would be for her daughter!

The bad news is Mom didn't tell Mary before Mary went on a deposition the next day.

The bad news is that once the deposition commenced, the computer started acting a little strange.

The bad news is that the computer burst into flame.

The good news is that Mary and the attorneys put the fire out without harm to life or limb.

The bad news is that the potential 200-page 0+3 turned into a 100-page oh-my-God.

The good news is that Mary had all of her other work backed up on floppy disks (this was a few years ago).

The best news is that Mom gladly and humbly replaced Mary's computer with a new, even better model, and thereafter stuck to helping with the housework.

From Cornfields to Courtrooms

By Daniel Feldhaus, RPR, CRR, RMR

When I was in high school, if you had told me that I would one day be a court reporter, I would have laughed. As a senior in 1978, my career path seemed so crystal clear: I would be a farmer like my father, and like his father before him. (My plan for a fallback job? Dirt-track motorcycle racer like Bubba Shobert, racing on soft-cushion dirt tracks). But life has an interesting way of transporting a shy farm kid from South Dakota to the big cities of Reno, Nevada, and Sacramento, California.

In high school, I found three skills I really excelled in: wrestling, playing trumpet, and typing. A teacher suggested that I consider court reporting as a career. My thoughts: *"What the heck is court reporting? Never heard of it.*" It didn't seem like a promising idea. But when I heard that the female-male ratio at the nearest reporting school was 35 to 1, I was *persuaded* that it might be worth a shot.

I later discovered that my vision of the gender advantage at court reporting school did not jibe with reality. Notwithstanding, it got me to the big city of Sioux Falls, where I learned to be a court reporter.

In the back of my mind, I still thought I would be a farmer because I loved the freedom of living in wide-open spaces and riding my motorcycle. I just couldn't imagine working indoors for the rest of my life. But I figured that until I decided to settle down and become a farmer, court reporting provided me with ample gas money for racing bikes.

What didn't really dawn on me until after court reporting school was that most reporting jobs moved the reporter away from wide-open spaces, into cramped, busy cities. That was something of a culture shock that I had to deal with.

When I began my reporting career, my assumptions about the sanctity and solemnity of the written word, the testimony of a witness, drove me to work very hard at my craft. My 19-year-old brain actually feared that if I made a mistake in my transcript – if I couldn't keep up and I dropped testimony – maybe I would be thrown in prison. Not county jail, but maximum security prison, because making a mistake in a transcript was a violation of the sanctity of my duty as a court reporter, and that the lives and livelihoods of litigants depended on my record.

I was living in Reno at the beginning of my career, and I felt sure that if I were thrown in prison as a result of my failure to perform satisfactorily, my family living in South Dakota wouldn't visit me because I would be so far away, and airline tickets were pretty hefty. The thought of living the rest of my days in the slammer (and waking in my lonely cell from a nightmare where I emphatically tell the judge that I thought I heard the witness say *doggy-dog world* and not *dog-eat-dog world)* pushed me to work hard – often into the wee hours of the morning.

This irrational fear turned out to be very useful, as it drove me to work very hard on my theory and my briefs. I feverishly learned to master my machine and the various ways to squeeze speed and accuracy out of those 23 keys. And that is a good thing.

Today, I still challenge myself to improve my writing. Even in the most mundane reporting assignment, for example, I create briefs for common, everyday phrases in my job. Each day, I strive to be a better reporter than the previous day. And that is a good thing.

After 31 years of reporting, although I still miss life on the farm, I absolutely love my profession and wouldn't want to do anything else. And that is a *very* good thing.

Daniel Feldhaus, RPR, RMR, CRR, began his court reporting career in 1980, and has worked in South Dakota, Nevada, and California.

He is a past president of the Northern California Court Reporters Association, and has won the California state speed contest. Dan has also placed nationally in both the speed and realtime competitions.

He and his wife, Cathy, reside in Sacramento. As Dan does not consider farming to ever be in his professional future, the growing of tomatoes and strawberries in the back yard is left to Cathy.

Realtime Is Better than You Think

By Joseph O. Inquagiato, RPR, RMR, CSR

Long before realtime translation became commonplace, I was asked by a good client to provide realtime for a deposition involving the investment of funds by their client, a speaking deaf person.

Up to this point in my career, I had never attempted realtime. I had, however, spent countless hours eliminating the conflicts from my dictionary when I made the switch from manual to computer-assisted transcription after 20 years of reporting, practicing every night as if I were trying to pass a 240 literary test.

I wasn't convinced that this would be beneficial for a non-hearing person. There would be numbers galore. There would be untranslates and mistranslates. The text would be completely unedited. I just couldn't see how it would be helpful. Still, I agreed to try.

As the deposition began, just as I had feared, the testimony came in fast and fierce, full of complex numbers and proper names. I knew I wasn't writing perfectly, but I pushed as hard as I could and hoped it would be enough for the gentleman to follow along. At the end of the deposition, he and his counsel left without speaking to me, and my heart sank. "Well," I thought, "I did the best job I could. I guess realtime isn't all it's cracked up to be."

Two days later, I received a letter of thanks from the plaintiff, expressing amazement at how well the realtime had worked. He stated that this was the first time since losing his hearing that he had been able to fully participate in a group discussion.

In that moment, I understood both the possibilities and the impact this technology would have, not only on bench and bar, but in the communities in which we live and work. From that point on, I began to encourage and guide my fellow reporters in readying themselves for the realtime revolution, and I never looked back.

Vignette 12: X-Rated Reporting

By Jack Boenau, RPR, CRR, CBC, CCP, RDR, FAPR

There's not a better time to talk about "war stories" in this fascinating profession than after reminiscing with other reporters. Having worked in conventions, as a freelancer, an official, and a captioner, I have seen plenty.

When I was very new to court reporting, I was given some interesting assignments for a 19- or 20-year-old neophyte, starting with reporting the trials of temporary injunctions against some new XXX-rated theaters. The judge was afraid the theater owner would edit the film before the actual trial, so he scheduled a viewing in the theater with the county solicitor, police, and lots of "interested citizens," so many, in fact, that subsequent hearings were held at the Orlando Naval Base where these citizens would have to show ID to get in.

The judge told me that I was to report everything in the films, including descriptions of what was taking place when there was little or no conversation, and that I may have to read my notes back to the jury. As it turned out, I didn't have to appear before a jury.

With that experience subsumed in my resume, I must have been seen as the right choice – maybe the only choice – to handle the hearings and trial involving the famous red-headed stripper, Tempest Storm, whose age and measurements were often mixed up in the media. It was another popular story that ran for months.

And while she was busted on several charges, the law was found to be unconstitutional, and she was pronounced free to perform. And this young reporter survived another early test in his career.

Reporter Adventures: The Henley Miniseries

By Susan Goldstein Henley, RPR, CRR, CBC, CCP, RDR, FAPR

When I am asked what I do for a living and I say that I am a court reporter, the initial intrigue or curiosity quickly fades when I say I am a freelancer and I do not work in court. It seems the general public cannot fathom my job happening anywhere but in the courtrooms of their favorite TV legal dramas.

Working as a freelance court reporter since 1973 and, of late, as a CART provider or captioner, my career has put me in some of the best and worst places and situations one could imagine. My mind floats through my experience and lightly lands on a few choice moments.

Chapter 1: The Seagulls Drowned Out the Testimony

I had to take the deposition of a man out on a pier at the wharf in Galveston, Texas because he would not go into "any of them fancy offices with no fresh air."

I was given a choice of sitting on either a huge, empty wooden cable spool, or in a golf cart. I chose the spool because it did not sway in the wind like the golf cart did on its spongy tires. Either way, this was going to be a reporting challenge.

My client, the defense attorney, had to put a hand over my paper tray so that the wind wouldn't take my notes away while I wrote. Yes, this was before paperless writers! Things went along smoothly, only stopping here and there for the loud horns of the ships entering and exiting the port.

Chapter 2: The Reporter as Landlubber

I was assigned to take the deposition of a ship's captain in his quarters aboard ship. We were tied to the dock, so that gave me a measure of comfort.

The engine was being repaired and was repeatedly revved, over and over and over, causing the ship to rock back and forth in the water. I became very seasick and as green as a pea.

It was a great story for my client to tell, the deposition where the court reporter became seasick and we weren't even at sea.

Chapter 3: Auto Reporting Skill

I took the deposition of a witness in a parking lot, in the back seat of her car, because she was too scared to enter the building.

Chapter 4: Not Deaf, Not Dumb

A plaintiff in a personal injury case was being deposed, and the questioning attorney asked the witness a typical, obvious question: "Where were you injured?"

The witness pointed to the middle finger on his right hand and said, "There."

The lawyer attempted to explain to the man that he had to repeat his answer out loud for the benefit of the court reporter, that the description needed to be more accurate for her record.

The witness became increasingly impatient, waiting for the attorney's instruction to end, and finally blurted out, "Right there! Is she *blind*, too?"

Chapter 5: Korean Isn't That Hard to Learn

I was doing a deposition in Korea through an interpreter utilizing a realtime screen, because the phraseology of

Korean speech was such that the interpreter needed the complete question before him in order to interpret it for the witness. The witness was answering, in Korean, "I don't know," to just about every question.

Well, we all know how painfully slowly interpreted testimony proceeds, and how our minds tend to wander, how we do mental exercises, anything to stay awake.

I heard the witness state in Korean, "I don't know," and reflexively wrote it in English before the interpreter had a chance to translate. It caught the interpreter so off-guard to see the answer in English before he had translated it that he burst out laughing, something not usually done in the Korean culture in a proper business setting. The rest of us laughed as well. I was definitely more alert after that!

Chapter 6: The Best of the Breast

A reporter I work with was covering a baseball game for me, providing open captioning to the jumbo board at Minute Maid Park in Houston. One of the promo spots she wrote should have read, "These lucky fans have just won four tickets in the dugout seats," but, instead it read, "These lucky fans have just won four tits in the dugout seats."

Each letter on this particular board is approximately four feet high by three feet wide, and shows to an audience of up to 42,000 people. Needless to say, aside from the stadium erupting in laughter, the guys in video operations pleaded with her to "do it again!"

 *Susan Goldstein Henley, RPR, CRR, CBC, CCP, RDR, FAPR, has been reporting for over 35 years, and presently is a CART provider with Allied Advanced Reporting in Houston, Texas. She has presented motivational and technical seminars on the subjects of writing realtime, CART, and speedbuilding.*

Susan is the winner of the Texas Court Reporters Association speed contest, as well as the Houston Court Reporters Association realtime contest. She is also a three-time medalist in the National Court Reporters Association speed contest.

Susan is a past director of the TCRA, as well as of the TCRA CART Foundation. She has also served in the past as president of the HCRA and president of the Bay Area Court Reporters Association of Texas.

A Nauseating Experience

By Michelle Vitrano, RPR, RMR, RDR, CRR, CBC

The day started out like any other day in Superior Court. We were going to continue taking testimony in a first-degree murder trial where a man was accused of shooting his wife square between the eyes. State witnesses had been put up for several days, and now it was the defendant's turn to take the stand in his own defense to explain what had happened.

He was explaining that he was in the living room with his wife, whom he loved very much. He decided to clean his gun on that quiet Sunday afternoon while the two of them enjoyed each other's company. He claimed that the gun went off accidentally.

The defendant had been in a car accident shortly before the trial started and was wearing a restrictive neck brace while on the witness stand. He was very upset and emotional while recounting the events of the day of the shooting.

During his testimony, one of the attorneys requested a sidebar conference with the judge to argue an objection outside the presence of the jury. While counsel and the Court were at sidebar, I began to edit on my computer. In our jurisdiction, sidebar conferences are not reported.

Out of the corner of my eye, I could see the defendant making what I feared was the universal gagging motion. I was the only one close enough to him to take action, so I quickly grabbed the small trashcan at my station and shoved it toward him just in time to catch the voluminous vomitus before it hit the taxpayer-funded carpet. It felt like a scene out of a Monty Python movie. A few jurors and observers witnessed this courtroom mini-drama, but the judge and attorneys, deeply focused on their confidential discussion, were oblivious.

I calmly put the trash can down and walked over to the side of the bench. In spite of the fact that my heart was racing and my nostrils were flaring as a result of the incident, I calmly explained to the sidebar participants what had just occurred.

I am heartily proud to say that I did not have a drop of vomit anywhere on me. It was a perfect catch. My motherly skill and nerves of steel resulted in not only fully rescued flooring, but also at the same time upheld courtroom decorum.

Many of my colleagues found out what happened and I was teased unmercifully. The next day a fellow reporter burst into my courtroom, excitedly clutching an article from the *Eastside Journal* detailing the previous day's nauseating events. My heroic puke capture was, in my humble opinion, the highlight of the newspaper piece.

Well, all in a day's work. There was no need to thank me. There are things that can happen any day in a court reporter's life that no schooling can prepare you for. I love being a court reporter. There isn't anything else I would want to be doing.

Human behavior is so unpredictable. I think that is why I love being an official in court. Every day is different.

And I deeply appreciate all of the highly sophisticated equipment and tools that being a court reporter mandates that we have in order to do a fully professional job...including a trash can.

Michelle Vitrano, RPR, RMR, CRR, CBC started school at the Academy of Court Reporting in 1982. She received her California CSR in 1985 at the ripe young age of 21, and began working at a large freelance firm in San Diego.

In 1988, she moved to Seattle, WA to take the position of Director of Education at the Court Reporting Institute while freelancing part-time. In 1990, Michelle accepted a position as an official court reporter with King County Superior Court in Seattle, and has more than 21 years of service there.

May I Have Your Autograph?

By Regina A. Berenato-Tell, RPR, RMR, CRR

They say that everyone gets their 15 minutes of fame...

The judge I was assigned to had a good mix of really interesting cases. We worked well together, I felt, and one day in 2003 as we were chatting, I asked her if she had ever seen realtime. She replied, "Well, they gave me LiveNote because I have this mass tort case they just assigned to me, but I don't really know what it is or how to use it."

Mass tort? *What the heck is a mass tort*, I remember thinking...

The next opportunity I had, I hooked myself into the judge's laptop to show her realtime, and from the very instant she saw it, she was hooked. I never realized that, just by showing her this technology, my career path would change so drastically.

In September of 2005 it was time to take that "mass tort" to trial that we had first talked about a few years earlier. It had become apparent to me that this was a pretty important case. Monthly case management conferences were held wherein a minimum of 50 attorneys from all across the country would attend. Issues were so hotly contested, arguing over every detail was the norm. Big money was at stake – I take that back; not big money, HUGE money.

The first morning of the trial, I thought I was going to faint. I walked up to the courthouse only to see the streets lined with news vans, reporters standing everywhere, mics in hand, just waiting for someone to pounce on. I quickly slipped in the side door, ran up to my office, shut the door and counted backwards from 10, taking deep breaths. This was it. I had to put all my nerves aside and get in there and do my job, which wasn't going to be an easy thing to do under the microscope of the media, TV cameras everywhere, reporters buzzing around constantly.

And did I mention that technically this was the most difficult case I had ever reported in my career? Not only did I have to provide a near-perfect realtime feed, I had to provide transcripts to attorneys who were waiting on pins and needles for my record. Associates and partners alike would start e-mailing me incessantly around 10:00 p.m., "Where's the transcript, Regina? We need it NOW!"

There was a reporter from *The Wall Street Journal* who had always been very friendly to me throughout the trial, always had a "good morning" for me, and just generally seemed to be a nice person. All my career, I was taught that you never speak to the media, so I knew to keep my distance.

One day she approached me and asked me if I would please let her interview me. I politely declined, telling her that I had no opinion on the case and I did not give interviews...ever. "No," she said, "I want to talk to you about what it's like to be a court reporter."

I was flattered, but still not so sure it was the right thing to do. What if she twisted my words or put a different spin on things I said? I thought about it long and hard, and decided that it could possibly be good for the court reporting profession if I did talk to her about my career.

My story ran in *The Wall Street Journal* in the *"It's a Living"* section, and I can say that the reporter did a great job. It gave me a great sense of pride and accomplishment to be able to shed a favorable light on our profession in such a huge publication. (I think my father bought out every issue within a 20-mile radius of my home town!)

I've continued to report for the same judge, and we've moved on to other mass torts since our first one, but we love to reminisce and think back to our first one. It was a tremendous experience.

Regina A. Berenato-Tell, RPR, RMR, CRR, CCR, has been happily reporting since her 1987 graduation from Peirce College in Philadelphia, Pennsylvania. She is employed as an official realtime court reporter for the Superior Court of New Jersey in Atlantic County, having reported for the Hon. Carol E. Higbee,  *Presiding Judge Civil, for the past eight years.*

She has also worked for the Superior Court of Delaware in Wilmington, Delaware as well as for numerous freelance agencies in the Delaware/Pennsylvania/New Jersey area.

Regina is the immediate past president of the Certified Court Reporters Association of New Jersey, and serves on several committees and task forces of the National Court Reporters Association.

You Should Maybe Stick to Happy Hanukkah

By Maxyne G. Bursky, BA, RPR, CRR, CCR

The clock on the wall was quickly heading for 5:30 on a sunny weekday afternoon in Fort Lauderdale, Florida. I was finishing up proofing a massive daily deposition from the day before when my buddy Tamara dragged herself in. She was exhausted from a full day of what she described as a difficult and contentious depo.

I perceived that she wanted to invite me to her pity party, so I asked her to wait five minutes while I did a spell-check, and I would gladly join her in a massive whinefest. Tamara agreed, and got us both a diet soda. She then proceeded to wax eloquent about the attorneys who refused to take a breath, the witness who mumbled more than enunciated, and the ultimate problem – the Yiddish and Hebrew words and phrases that were thrown around.

Tamara's issue was that she was a nice, Irish Catholic girl who had heard a few words (*mazel tov, shmuck*) from Eastern European Judaic culture used in everyday conversation, but both attorneys and the witness were Jewish, and there were several phrases bandied about that were literally foreign to her. She set up her computer and searched for the arbitrary stroke she hit every time a new strange phrase came up, and asked me its meaning and a possible spelling. Then she came to the most perplexing portion of the depo.

"Oh, this is something that I really don't know how to handle. It doesn't make sense to me, but I *know* I heard it," her brows knitted together in perplexed concern. "It's not a Jewish phrase, but it has something to do with Rosh Hashana. And it's really gross."

I had no earthly idea what she was talking about. As I sipped my soft drink, I listened to the story unfold, and nearly choked when she concluded.

"The witness said he was president of the temple he belonged to, and he was given the honor every year at the service to *blow the chauffeur*. I know the guy is rich and all, but I can't figure this out. Is that *really* a custom?"

Once I was able to pick my jaw up off the floor, I read aloud the testimony I saw on her screen that concerned the witness and the alleged unfortunate limo driver. Then it dawned on me.

The ram's horn is traditionally sounded as a herald of the Jewish New Year, or Rosh Hashana. To be chosen to blow the horn is a great honor — a *mitzvah* — and apparently, the witness was among the privileged few at his synagogue.

The Hebrew word for the ram's horn is *shofar*, pronounced one of two ways, either SHOW-FAR or SHOW-FER.

It was glorious to see the relief on Tamara's face when she realized that my religious preference didn't include kinky holiday traditions.

Depos to the Left, Depos to the Right...

By Kenneth McClure, RPR, RMR

If you didn't have an all-day assignment as a freelancer with some serious degree of seniority, you were likely to have a 10:00 and then a 2:00. This was largely hypothetical. Who knows how long a deposition will really last? But this long-ago 1980 day contained a predictable fly in the scheduling ointment, a morning deposition in Manhattan Supreme Court and an afternoon EBT (examination before trial) in Brooklyn Supreme Court.

The distance between the sites wasn't the problem. In this time before laptops, you could fold up your steno machine at 60 Centre Street in downtown New York City proper and have it set up in a neighboring borough in all of 30 minutes, thanks to the swiftly efficient public transportation system. But the courthouses did not welcome and seemed designed to frustrate depositions.

Lawyers persisted in holding them there because the buildings harbored judges who could direct witnesses to answer questions that their attorneys had instructed them not to. In Manhattan, suitable rooms were so scarce that, unless all parties were there early, you could wait hours to start.

Wily reporters could sometimes covertly shepherd their parties to recondite jury rooms, hidden in the building's labyrinthian interior, where depositions might be held. At other times, actual juries were there ensconced, and the freelancer's accommodation attempt would be thwarted.

This day, there was just no room at the inn, and around 11:30, desperate for a manger where our depo might be born, we set down on a bench outside the courthouse, midst the sounds of the throbbing city, and the parties present commenced yelling. After the wind whipped my steno paper out of its tray, the defending attorney graciously spent the duration of the proceeding with his hand securing it.

In no less than three instances, sirens that could not be competed with forced us to pause. Nevertheless, by 12:30, I was packed up and on my way to Brooklyn.

You would not usually get shut out in Brooklyn. You could almost always get a table; in one cavernous room there were about 16 of them. But with several depositions being conducted within immediate earshot of the reporter, the challenge was to keep the doctor's testimony from conflating with the economist's at the neighboring table about two feet away, or the driver's immediately behind. There was always the threat of something like: "Q. To a reasonable degree of medical certainty, what is the expected working life of the average 58-year-old fiscal year when you first saw the Smith vehicle?"

On this day in particular, things degraded fast. The alarm in this chasmal room commenced blaring, holding us in the authoritative grip of its warning. It was a faux fire drill, we were told almost immediately.

"Don't worry about it," the clerk shouted over the blare. Sixteen depositions continued unabated, everyone shouting apace.

This vast depo space was often put to other uses (simultaneously with examinations being conducted). When Brooklyn street people, eschewing their medication, flipped out spectacularly, they would be led to a corner of the cavern to be processed.

About five minutes into the blaring of the fire alarm, a breathtakingly unmedicated homeless man was led into the room, legs shackled but lingually unfettered, screaming to beat the cacophonous band. When his unfocused rage intermittently found articulable expression, he could be heard to repeatedly intone – and you could not help but hear him, even above the alarm – "I'm gonna kill all of you (expletive-deleted)!"

Undeterred, the 16 deponents continued to testify, and 16 dedicated court reporters continued to pound the keys of their steno machines, in short order producing beautifully unconflated transcripts, betraying no hint of the chaos that lurked just at the edges of their four corners.

The Future is Now

By Merilyn Sanchez, RPR, RMR, CRR, FAPR

As I reflect back on my 30-plus years in the court reporting field, there are so many memories of the friends, the opportunities, and the growth this profession has provided me. I think the one memory that stands out most in my mind is the time, on behalf of our profession, I impressed a Supreme Court Justice.

I was fortunate to have been chosen in 1986 by NCRA to work in one of their three sponsored Courtrooms of the Future. Realtime technology was relatively new at that time, and NCRA wisely predicted that it would be realtime that would differentiate us from electronic recording and keep reporters in the courtroom. Everyone was skeptical – from the judges and court administrators to my fellow court reporters. How could this technology benefit anyone? Why would they want to spend money on computers for the judges in the courtroom? How in the world would an official reporter write realtime all day long? We decided the best way to promote court reporters and realtime technology would be to demonstrate its usefulness every day.

Computers and monitors were installed in Judge Roger Strand's courtroom at the judge's bench and at each counsel table. In the early stages, the participants could only read what was scrolling on the monitors, but as the hardware and software developed, we added litigation support software and they were all able to mark, annotate, and issue-code the realtime transcript. I provided realtime viewing for free to the attorneys on an "experimental basis" from 1986 until 2001, when all of the reporters in my district started writing everything in realtime for their judges. After that, the attorneys no longer had realtime unless they paid for it.

Judge Strand and I gave over 250 demonstrations of our Courtroom of the Future, which later became known as the Computer-Integrated Courtroom. Few were as nerve-racking for me as the time Supreme Court Chief Justice Rehnquist and the head of the FBI, William

Sessions, came to see what this new technology was all about.

Judge Strand entertained them with courtroom war stories, and I endeavored to write my best realtime ever, including the city of Tegucigalpa coming up perfectly. (Of course, we had done this before and I knew the word would be coming up.) Both dignitaries watched the screen intently, but didn't visibly react to what they were seeing.

I had a scopist in my office editing as I was writing, and then printing the pages as she finished them. Justice Rehnquist and Judge Sessions left the courtroom for a brief tour of Judge Strand's chambers before heading to their next meeting. They were in chambers probably less than five minutes. I patiently waited at the elevators with printed and bound copies of our hour-long presentation.

They recognized me from the courtroom and thanked me for the demonstration. The looks on their faces were absolutely priceless when I thanked them for coming and handed them a copy of the demonstration. I don't think they knew what it was at first. When I explained to them that it was a transcript of what had just transpired in the courtroom, they exclaimed, "Wow, that's impressive." Judge Sessions indicated he wished he had had that available when he was on the bench.

It certainly doesn't happen often, and it probably isn't easy to impress such high-ranking individuals, but I think I managed to do it that day. Every day at work as a court reporter provides the opportunity to work hard, learn something new, and sometimes even to dazzle the participants.

Merilyn Sanchez, RPR, RMR, CRR, FAPR, has been a court reporter for over 30 years. She presently works in Phoenix, Arizona.

Merilyn has presented seminars on court technology, and has led People to People delegations to China, Russian, South Africa, and

 *Israel to advocate for the court reporting profession. She is a past president of the National Shorthand Reporters Association.*

Epilogue

By Kenneth McClure, RPR, RMR

In the postmodern world, we're less sure of things than we used to be. This can be discussed in ethereally highfalutin ways that, say, expound the philosophical implications of Heisenberg's uncertainty principle. But a court reporter, whose pedestrian business is to wrestle spoken works into meaningful textual captivity, might hope to remain untroubled by such abstruse considerations. And yet they plague us.

Our world is apparently experienced in the subjunctive mood, throbbing with doubt. "That's, like, the only reason, you know, for these kind of sentences. You know what I'm saying?"

The locution, "you know," conspiratorially summons the listener to assent to whatever the speaker asserts. The fear that the listener may not know is betrayed when that brief expression spreads its wings into that pleaful interrogative, "You know what I'm saying?"

The ubiquitous "like" effectively takes the backbone out of factual assertions and dissolves them into metaphors. Either matters of fact do not exist as clearly as they once did, or we don't have the self-confidence, as we once did, to call them as we see them.

Maybe this is not such a big deal. It is true that reporters seeking to keep such utterances as meaningful as they can be kept, must forever set off this incoherent noise in commas. But they may be nothing more than mere fillers, as some linguists tell us they are, little more than a succession of nervous tics, blips in an otherwise perfectly intelligible statement.

And then there is upspeak, which seems to be the same kettle of odious fish.

Reporters, as custodians of meaning, are taught to reflet any interrogative inflection at the end of the sentence with a question mark. The difference can be vitally important.

It is one thing to say, "I killed him." It is another thing altogether to say, "I killed him?" Yet upspeakers habitually end their otherwise perfectly declarative sentences with an interrogative lilt. Every assertion is tentatively ventured, modulated into a revocable hypothesis, and offered to the listener who (as long as he does not speak upspeak) has the power to confirm or deny it.

We contemplate here a characterological disintegration; the speaker cannot summon a sufficient sense of self to make a factual assertion.

As court reporters, herding these spoken words into their place on the page, there is only so much we can do to make whole the hollow men and women who uttered them or to restore coherence to the postmodern world. As a practical matter, we are duty-bound to register that interrogative lilt and let the chips fall where they may. But as a citizen of the world, this is an occasion of great pain for the reporter who is positioned to appreciate what his contemporaries do not fully comprehend.

This is, you know, like, the way the world ends, not with a bang but a whimper? You know what I'm saying? You know what I'm saying.

About Maxyne G. Bursky, BA, RPR, CRR, CCR

Maxyne has been a court reporter for more than 33 years. She has freelanced out of the Atlanta area for the past six years. She is a certified performance coach, having mentored many students. Maxyne has worked as a freelancer in New York and Florida as well as in the US District Court for the Southern District of NY.

In addition to **Way Off the Record,** she has written **Talk to the Hands**, a humorous, practical guide for the newbie reporter that provides easy, yet comprehensive ways to navigate the world of court reporting that are almost never taught in schools, and allows a nervous newcomer to this exciting field to feel more like a veteran. Another helpful booklet, **The *Term*-inator**, was written by Maxyne as a quick reference to give reporters in the early part of their careers a leg up on the most common terms of art used in medical, legal, industrial, and other areas.

Maxyne lectures on the joy of court reporting to both steno and voice students and young professionals, and is a participant in the Virtual Mentor program sponsored by the NCRA. She is also a member of the board of Casey's Kids, an organization dedicated to providing books and supplies to Title I public schools. She has been actively involved in dog rescue for over 15 years. Her book, **Good Dogs with Bad Names**, has raised money for various animal charities.

Way Off the Record is donating a portion of the profits from every book sold to the NCRA Foundation and the Hallyboy Foundation to provide scholarships for reporting students.